Praise for

Unemployable: How AI Transformed My Work and Life

"An inspiring story of grit, determination, and ambition balanced with kindness, generosity, and passion. Read this book and learn what it takes to make your dreams come true."

—John Spence, business leader and executive coach

"Disarmingly candid and brutally honest all at once, Alysia's memoir-cum-life reflection book reads like a fireside conversation with your wise and chatty friend. Inspiring and entertaining, quoting Steve Jobs and the Wizard of Oz in the same breath and sharing tales of hardship and clear-eyed realisations, *Unemployable* is a boundlessly enjoyable read."

—Mohamed El Dahshan, senior Economic Advisor, United Nations

"A lovely read that is magically a memoir, self-help, and career guidance book all in one. Alysia shares an entirely fresh perspective on finding purpose, passion, and success in life while seamlessly integrated practical tips for entrepreneurs. A must read for anyone looking for more sparkle in their career and life journey."

—Lauren Friedman Stat, Public Board director and entrepreneur

"The shortest distance between two people is a great story. This one is incredible. You will embrace this book like a friend you won't want to leave."

—Bob Dotson, Emmy Award winning *New York Times* Best Selling Author

"From her early days selling suits on the streets of Johannesburg, to her rise as a leading venture capitalist in Silicon Valley, Alysia shares her story of pain, perseverance, love, and the pursuit of the American Dream. Get ready for the ride of your life!"

—Jyoti Rai, business leader

"Exceptional! Alysia Silberg's journey and ability to transcend her environment and limited resources will inspire and uplift not only entrepreneurs and business owners but anyone that wakes up with thoughts that their situation is too tough and unsurmountable."

—Shirley Cress Dudley, best-selling author

"Every once in a while comes a book that entrepreneurs should read for inspiration and motivation. This is one of these books. Grab a copy for yourself and maybe an extra copy for a friend who is going through challenging times. You'll be glad you did!"

—Tripp Braden, Strategic Performance Partners Managing Partner

"Alysia's story is one of true grit, determination, and perseverance. It's an inspiration to so many entrepreneurs who defy the naysayers in life. Alysia sets us all on the right course in life!"

—Jeff Goldman, Emmy award winning retired CBS News White House Producer

"A truly inspirational story of grit and determination, reminding you to follow that rainbow and never listen to the naysayers. Thank you for reminding me what a blessing it is to be *Unemployable*."

—Mike Fannin, Entrepreneur and dreamer

"Once I started reading, I could not stop. The pages seemed to flip themselves. I was completely enthralled by Alysia's story as it unfolded. Hidden in plain sight are the lessons we all need to learn to be successful."

—Tony Bodoh, CEO of Tony Bodoh International,
a customer experience consultancy

"Alysia has done a masterful job of capturing her life's story and the adversity she faced while rising up into her career in Silicon Valley. It's a great read to gain insights into the type of persistence it takes to succeed in a global economy."

—Lane M. Campbell, serial entrepreneur

"Alysia Silbeg is a force of nature. Her path from the broken streets of South Africa, to a technology maven, is a clear reminder that it's not what happens to you that matters, but rather your response that counts most. Keep this book close, the lessons contained are powerful and profound."

—John St. Augustine, writer, consultant, and tech professional

"A personal and powerful read. The journey is full of twists, turns, and insights. Life isn't easy but in this inspiring book you will even find reasons for celebrating the difficult. What a story!"

—Greg Zlevor, President of Westwood International and
Founder of HopeMakers

"A magnificent woman, a magnificent journey, a story magnificently shared – illuminating, invigorating, inspirational."

—Amy Trask, sports analyst, author, and former CEO of the
Oakland Raiders

"Alysia Silberg's book is a must-read for anyone who is interested in the world of tech entrepreneurship. She has a gift for explaining complex concepts in simple terms, making her book accessible to readers with varying levels of experience. Her practical advice is invaluable for anyone who wants to start or grow a business."

—Ethan Pierse, Co-Founder, NFT Factory Paris.
Partner, Borderless Ventures

"Alysia is one of the little known true polymaths of the 21st century. Real Estate operator, educator, entrepreneur, investor, podcaster, institutional asset manager and more. Raw intelligence and grit ooze from every page as Alysia makes it look easier than you might reasonably believe.

"This book is a repackaging of Alysia's amazing life into a series of parables. The key to the book is not the lesson in each chapter, as much as it is the thought process taking place as Alysia faces and conquers her challenges along the way. Her thoughts are often written quietly, tucked between the lines, to be inferred from her actions.

"The book opens with Alysia thrust into a world of crumbling empires, which she tackles with great ferocity. By the latter stages, like Alexander the Great, many would feel there are no worlds left to conquer. I suspect Alysia is just getting started, and has a suitable second act to come."

—James West, CEO Globe Derivatives Exchange

"One of the top, most energetic, and crazy minds in Silicon Valley, with an even crazier story. It was hard to put the book down."

—Dan Jones, CEO, Debt Destroyed

"Alysia is one of the most compassionate, skillful, and visionary weavers of people and important ideas around her. She has an incredible taste for recognizing the signs of wise and powerful ways of thinking in founders and follows through in supporting them, even when they're out of the popular paradigm.

"Her crackling vivacity shines through everything she does, magnetizing incredible people. She channels her expansive creative energy with contemplative and restorative practices. She is a wonderful role model for how to live an integrated life as a highly creative person (like many of the founders she works with)!"

—Jacob Cole, CEO & Cofounder at Ideaflow

"It's an addictive read that you can't put down!"

—Nikola Parque, Entrepreneur

"She lands in our lives on a yet to be discovered, invented, transcending spaceship. Welcome to the wild ride of a woman from the future."

—Fabio Borges

"Look up 'vivacious, determined, informative and engaging' in the encyclopaedia, and there is a picture of Alysia Silberg. Read this book if you want inspiration to be and continue as an entrepreneur and company builder."

—John Abeles, venture investor, director, consultant, entrepreneur, and philanthropist, president and founder of MedVest, Inc.

UNEMPLOYABLE

How AI Transformed My Work and Life

UNEMPLOYABLE

How AI Transformed My Work and Life

Alysia Silberg

Foreword by Tim Draper

For information about special discounts for bulk purchases, please
email bulksales@alysiasilberg.com. For more information or to book the
author for a live event, please email speakerinfo@alysiasilberg.com

Foreword by Tim Draper

*Cover design and Illustrations by Alexander Londo with the assistance of
DALL·E 2, AI*

Library of Congress Control Number: 2023905793

Printed in the United States of America
Street Global Publishing, Howland Canal, Venice, CA 90291

ISBN: 979-8-9879877-0-4 (Hardcover)
979-8-9879877-1 (Paperback)
979-8-9879877-2-8 (eBook)
979-8-3507-0628-4 (Audiobook)

To Darren

Be Brave. Be True. Be You. Be Great. I love you.

Contents

Foreword
by Tim Draper

The world change meter is spinning exponentially faster now. With ChatGPT, people now understand that everyone's job is going to become more abstract, less mundane and more open to new horizons. When AI starts outperforming the average doctor (with Cloudmedx), the average lawyer (with LawTrades), the average software engineer (with ChatGPT), there is no job that won't go through some sort of a transformation. I fully expect AI to become better than the average VC in a year or two. In fact, if you combine a Singapore company called Seer that reads emotions and detects lies, with common questions, transcriptions and interpretations from a Silicon Valley company called Otter, and add in some broad search tools for due diligence on the people and the industry, I fully expect to start using AI to at least supplement my decision making in VC.

Add to this the transformation in the works around Bitcoin, where Bitcoin becomes the currency of the world, the blockchain collects taxes and keeps track of all debits and credits, NFT's keep records honest on what is a Rolex and what is a Rothko, smart contracts make agreements stick without legal maneuvering, and DAO's begin to transform everything from the insurance industry to jury participation, and you start to see how much change we will all be experiencing in the roaring 2020's.

In fact, space, transportation, robotics, medicine, real estate, nearly every industry in the world is going to go through a rapid change, so what is a startup to do?

Drive the change. The world is yours to mold. While you will need to react to new developments around the world, you will also be the architect of the industry you are building.

Think exponentially. Progress isn't linear. It is exponential. Every new breakthrough brings forward a new base from which people can innovate, and they do. So make sure your company can thrive through multiple technological doublings. If you hope to hit it big in 7 years, you have to be more than 100 times as good as what is out there today.

Stay alive. There will be tough times where cash is short. Use these times to build a "cockroach" culture. As my son Adam says, "Cockroaches don't die." So don't die. Conserve your cash. Keep your burn rate low. Often companies throw in the towel just a month or two before they get the big order that would have put them on the map.

Delight your customer. Ultimately it is your customer that is going to make you successful. Have an undying love for your customer. Bend over backwards to make him or her happy. Ask what he/she requires and try to anticipate his/her needs. A happy customer is your most effective sales force.

Enjoy the journey. Steve Jobs said a lot of things, but I think the best one is that he believed it wasn't the destination, but the journey that mattered. Entrepreneurship will take you to places you never thought you would go, physically, emotionally, spiritually and academically. The journey is the reward for all the work you put in.

Move the ball forward. Some of you will succeed and some will fail. Human progress grows in fits and starts. Know that even if you fail, you will have moved the ball forward. You will have shown a customer something new. You will have challenged your competitor to do a better job, You will have employed people on a mission they loved. Keep your ego in check. Your success as a human is not determined by how much Bitcoin you own. It is determined by how much better you leave this planet when you go.

This story of an adventurer and her adventures is a testament to the type of wayfarer the world needs right now — someone who is ambitious, determined, self-confident, restless and creative. Alysia Silberg has overcome great odds and has travelled far to get where she is today. We can all learn from her, as I have done from reading this book. Alysia, by her own definition, may be "unemployable", but more than that, she has proved herself to be unshakable in the pursuit of her dreams. This unputdownable book is the proof!

Live long and prosper.

Tim

Tim Draper is an American venture capital investor, and founder of Draper Fisher Jurvetson (DFJ), Draper University, and Draper Associates.

Prologue

It was a Saturday night. I was 15. My mom and I were just getting back from synagogue, heralding the end of Shabbat, the Jewish day of rest. The melody of an ancient song still rang in my ears, the plaintive notes connecting me to the hopes, devotions, and yearnings of generations past.

As our headlights swept the driveway of our home in the northern suburbs of Johannesburg, my brother, Richard, unlocked the heavy chain that secured our rusty gate. We couldn't afford a remote-controlled electric gate, as was common in our crime-plagued neighborhood. But we took what precautions we could.

A couple weeks before, I'd been paging through my granny's collection of women's magazines. An article in *Cosmopolitan* caught my eye. It was a list of things you should do to prevent yourself from becoming the victim of a carjacking.

Be vigilant. Be aware of your surroundings. Ask someone to meet you in the driveway. Park at an angle, so you can get away quickly should the need arise. Check your rearview and side-mirrors. Keep your doors locked, your windows closed. And if you come under attack, absolutely *do not resist*. Don't fight back. *Your life is worth more than your car.*

It wasn't the kind of article you might see in an American edition of *Cosmo*, but in South Africa, it was just another reminder of the rampant lawlessness plaguing our society. According to the piece, luxury vehicles such as BMWs and Mercedes were the most attractive targets, so in my mind, we were still relatively safe. After all, we drove a beaten-up old jalopy that was just about as rusty as our dilapidated gate.

Richard was standing next to the car. We rolled down the windows and were hit with a pungent chemical stench. We spent a moment in conversation, trying to ascertain what was causing this strange, eye-watering odor. Was it emanating from the engine? Or drifting over from a neighbor's backyard?

Then, to my horror, I remembered something else I had read just last week in the newspaper. A report on a terrible new trend in carjackings in our city. If a motorist resisted, the criminals would splash them with burning liquid. Hydrochloric Acid, or HCL—a highly corrosive fluid typically used to scour the walls of swimming pools.

I turned my head, catching the rush of shadows under a streetlamp, charging towards us.

I opened the door of the car.

And I screamed.

My mother—desperate to hold on to her most valuable, most prized possession—tightened her grip on the steering wheel. She knew exactly what was happening, but she wasn't going to let go.

Thud thud thud. As I would later discover, it was the sound of my mother being beaten in the face with the barrel of a gun.

The carjacker wrenched her from the driver's seat, threw her to the ground, kicked her, over and over again. My brother threw me to the ground as bullets flew.

I pushed myself up and ran to our neighbor's house, shouting for help. I felt a sharp, thudding pain in my side, but I kept on running, driven by fear and by adrenaline.

"Help! Somebody help! *Please help!*"

I stood outside their house, rattling the gate. Nobody came. Maybe no one was home. Maybe they were, and just didn't care.

We didn't even know our neighbors. In the suburbs of Joburg, houses are spaced apart and hidden behind high walls that are crowned with barbed or electrified wire. People keep to themselves. Many go so far as to disconnect their doorbells.

I reached to my side, tracing the source of the pain. I felt wetness. When I pulled back my hand, it was sticky with blood. I almost fainted.

The gate opened. Our neighbor, eyes wide with horror, beckoned me in.

"What's going on?"

I stumbled, dripping blood in the hallway. I saw the wash of blue light outside, as the police arrived, too late to do anything but take the testimonies of yet another crime in yet another suburb.

Later that night, I sat in the waiting-room of Johannesburg General Hospital, just another patient, just another emergency, on the busiest night of the week for blood, shock, and trauma. The ER doctor told me I was lucky. Lucky to have been struck in the hip by a stray bullet—lucky to be alive.

My mother was blinded in one eye by the pistol-whipping. Still, she somehow had the presence of mind to issue an ominous warning: "Don't say a word about this to anybody," she told me. "Don't tell your teachers, or any of the kids at school."

She didn't want us to be seen as weak. Defenseless. *Different* from all the rest. She didn't want us to be viewed as victims. We were to pretend that everything was okay. That everything was great. That we were doing just fine—even without my dad.

So I kept quiet. I lived with the pain. Nobody could see the scar

I carried. Nobody knew what was going through my head. All I could think of, in the days that followed, was the mantra you hear so often in Johannesburg: *This is no way to live.*

I wanted to run. I wanted to get as far away as possible from the land of my birth. I wanted to feel like a child again, free to wander, free to dream, free to be anyone I had ever wanted to be.

Free to be me.

ONE

Find Your Divine Sparkle

I'll never forget the first time I saw them. They were pretty and pink with black velvet stripes, and wheels that spun at the flick of my fingertips. Faster and faster, like the beating of my heart. I held them to my ear and listened to the whir. I pictured myself racing along the sidewalk, with a smile on my face and the wind in my hair. I was six years old, and I wanted those roller skates more than anything else in the world.

I sat on the floor in the sporting goods section of Hyperama, a huge warehouse store in my home city of Johannesburg, South Africa. I took off my shoes, revealing tatty socks, and slipped my feet in. A perfect fit. I felt like that poor little girl in the fairy tale, when the handsome prince finally catches up with her. I was Cinderella, and I was ready to roll.

"Alysia! Alysia!" I could hear my grandparents calling, from a few aisles down. The spell was broken. But my journey of dreams—the journey that would one day take me all the way to Silicon Valley—was only just beginning.

I took off the pretty pink roller skates and hid them at the back of the shelf. The price tag read: R19.99, at that time about $10 in American money. I knew I couldn't ask my grandparents to buy them for me. They could barely afford the groceries they were pushing around in their cart. Nor could I ask my mom and dad. Money was tight, the subject of constant worry and bickering. The closest I came to wealth was the scholarship I'd earned at my elite private school. I was going to have to find a way to pay for those skates.

Could I set up a lemonade stand on the front lawn of our house? Nope.

In our suburb, the houses had high walls crowned with electric fencing. The streets were patrolled by armed security guards because the police couldn't cope with the levels of crime. A kid with a business plan and a stash of coins would be asking for trouble.

But I had another idea.

My father liked to tell me that I was born with the gift of selling. "Alysia," he would say, "you were born with a divine sparkle. Never let it go." He said the light in my eyes reminded him of his favorite movie star, Marilyn Monroe. The way she could illuminate a room just by gliding into it, the glow she projected through the silver screen.

How could I ever hope to live up to that?

I was gawky and anxious, obsessed by math and calculus, stuck in a world of my own on the southern edge of the African continent. But to my father, Joe, *everyone* had the makings of a star. Everyone was born to shine. He was dazzled by the idea that we are defined by our dreams, all the more so because he was forced to let go of his own.

> *The streets were patrolled by armed security guards because the police couldn't cope with the levels of crime. A kid with a business plan and a stash of coins would be asking for trouble.*
> *But I had another idea.*

In Hollywood, where he worked as a make-up and special effects artist in the 1950s, he was on first-name terms with some of the biggest names on the marquee: not just Marilyn Monroe, but Natalie Wood, Marlon Brando, Yul Brynner, Grace Kelly, Fred Astaire, and many others. It was his job, using brushes and powders and paints and creams, to transform ordinary, everyday people, with all their secret fears and flaws, into icons and legends. In the kingdom of the imagination, he was an alchemist. And then—forced after years of following his dreams to return home and start a pharmacy in the central business district of Pretoria, the administrative capital of South Africa—he was just a chemist.

I was the odd kid out at school, shy, gawky, self-conscious of my less-than-privileged background. Looking back—that's me second from the right in the top row—I now realize that being different is what made all the difference.

He wore his white coat and stood behind the counter, crushing medicine with his pestle and mortar, filling and labeling the boxes and bottles that harbored the hope of healing. Pharmacy was his second calling, his backup plan, the comfortable cushion of a career that lay waiting when family pressure compelled him to return from the City of Dreams. His mother, recently widowed, kept begging him to come back home.

Stricken by guilt, weighed down by the burden of responsibility, he gave up his successful career in Hollywood. For many years, he cared for his mother, while building his pharmacy business from scratch. But even then, to tell the truth, Joe was never just a chemist.

When you walked through the doorway of Joe's Pharmacy,

you were also crossing the threshold to a world of fantasy and awe and wonder. It was a place where you could shed the shell of your lesser self and morph into a mirror-image of whoever you had always wanted to be. A wizard, a warrior, a vampire, a cowboy, an emperor, a sheik, a showgirl, a superhero, a Martian, a mad scientist, a monster, a zombie, a dancer in top hat and tails, and yes, maybe even Marilyn.

Because Joe's Pharmacy, dressed up in its own double-identity, was also Joe's Magical Costume Hire, the only two-in-one store of its kind in all the world.

My father could tell by instinct, by body language, by a *glance*, that a customer had come in to find a costume, rather than to fill a prescription. And then he himself would be transformed, quickening his step, widening his smile, steering the customer by the arm to his showroom of outfits and accessories, where anyone could be transformed into a star. He was especially proud of what he called his Mount Rushmore of Hollywood Heroes—the famous faces who gazed down from the tops of the medicine cabinets.

He would tell stories about the stars, how he'd known and worked with them, how he'd helped to make them look so glamorous, so heroic on the silver screen. "Now which Hollywood hero would you like to be today?" he'd ask his customers, and the lights in their eyes would shine.

But the magic would disappear the moment my mother walked in.

To her, the theatrical store was at best a gimmicky indulgence, at worst a tacky intrusion on the serious business of helping people get well. And making money. Always, making money.

A pharmacy was meant to be clean and clinical, with a single-minded devotion to health and wellness. But here there were piles of costumes and masks, and cobwebs and glitter all over the place. It was as if every day was Halloween, and the simple act of getting your medicine had been turned into a form of trick or treat. Even worse, in her eyes—as a chemist, he would often treat people, dispensing sometimes costly pharmaceuticals, without accepting payment.

His signature remedy was a cough mixture distilled from beeswax, and people would come from near and far to get a bottle. He was a tinkerer, an experimenter, an inventor, tirelessly toiling away with his flasks and formulas. From him, I inherited the curiosity that would one day lead me all the way to Silicon Valley.

"Oom Joe"—Uncle Joe, as his customers called him—would climb a rickety ladder to a high shelf, and would descend with the mixture in hand.

He would carefully explain how to use it—just a spoonful, a couple of times a day—and when the customer handed over the money, he would shrug it off: "Don't worry about it, just make good use of it!" The customer would feel better already, and my mother would be furious.

It was only many years later that I came to realize there may have been a deeper explanation for her fury. Her name was Joan. She was strikingly beautiful, with long red hair, blue eyes, and porcelain-white skin. In her youth, she'd been a prima ballerina, until a bad injury had clipped her wings. Like that famous swan in Tchaikovsky's ballet, she folded into herself, the exhilaration of the dance giving way to resentment at every reminder of the freedom she'd once had to fly.

Like many dancers, her grace and beauty on the stage concealed the torturous demands of her discipline. She starved herself to stay thin, exercised for hours a day, and locked herself in the bathroom at night. I would hear her throwing up, her body wasting away as her mind struggled to cope with the pain. And then, she would take it out on my father.

In one of my earliest memories, I am walking to the back of the shop. I am carefree and happy among all the costumes. It is my favorite place in the world. I'm five years old. From somewhere in the darkness, I hear a *thwacking* sound. I freeze in my tracks as I catch sight of something horrible. My mother, hitting my father—over the head and shoulders—again and again. She has a wooden hanger in her hand. My father is cowering, shielding his face. His mug of coffee goes flying. My mother is *screaming*. Even at that tender age, I know what it's all about—her fury, her unstoppable rage.

Money.

It was always the same, between them.

I knew the way my mother treated my father wasn't right. She became increasingly abusive to him, emotionally and physically.

No one could understand why. I still don't. I say all of this without malice or resentment, but because it's important in understanding where I come from, and the paths I've taken in life.

I would overhear my mother crying to my grandmother, telling her how she was married to "the poorest Jew in the world," which only worsened my grandmother's antisemitism. I would hear my mother shouting at my father about the money he owed, about his haphazard financial management, about his habit of giving customers costly medicines for nothing. He tried as hard as he could to make peace, to make light of all his troubles.

"What are they going to do," he would ask playfully, a fedora on his head, a fake cigar in his mouth, "drag me away like Al Capone?"

I never heard him bemoaning what could and would and should have been. It was enough that he had gone to Hollywood, that he had worked with the stars, that he had come to know them as friends. I never heard him, either, reflecting on his family's journey from Lithuania, after the pogroms, to seek refuge in a faraway land. He was a born storyteller, with an actor's flair for dramatization, but it was in his nature to look up, to the light, rather than back, into the darkness.

The stories he would tell me were stories of kings in their castles, of *Arabian Nights*, of *Peter and the Wolf*, with each instrument in the musical accompaniment representing a different character. In turn, I would have to come up with stories of my own. "So tell me, what did you learn today?" he would ask, every day after school.

I thought long and hard about my answers.

I wanted to appear worldly and wise and well-informed, so that in sharing my knowledge, my father would learn something too. But the real lessons, the lessons that would stay with me for life, were the lessons I learned while working in Joe's Pharmacy and Magical Costume Hire Store.

I was little more than a toddler when I began welcoming customers at the door, with a smile wide enough to reveal the gaps in my teeth. My father would let me grab hold of the pestle, and I would *crush, crush, crush*. I would sweep the floor and arrange the costumes in their racks and banish dust from the shelves. My dad was a fair employer. He paid me for my labor—just not enough to buy a pair of pretty pink roller skates with black velvet stripes. They were my dream, my goal, my prize. I knew I wouldn't stop until I held them in my hands.

But how?

I found the answer a few days after that shopping expedition with my grandparents, while I was hanging up men's suits in the costume section of my father's shop. They were 1970s-style outfits, tapered at the waist, with wide lapels and trousers that flared from the knee. They were the look of *Super Fly*, the 1972 movie about life on the streets in the underworld of Harlem.

My father had a rack of these suits in his cupboard at home. I had never seen him wear them, not even once.

What if I could put them up for sale?

I told my father my bright idea. He looked me in the eye and laughed. "Sure," he said. "Suit yourself!"

So one morning, I set up a table outside the drugstore, the suits neatly displayed in all their *Super Fly* glory. The store was in a lucky spot, right across from the police station and surrounded by government buildings. There was plenty of passing trade. I picked a busy day, propped up the sign, and meticulously arranged the suits and other items.

"Roll up, roll up!" I shouted, ringing the big brass bell, like Father Christmas. "Big sale today! Don't miss out! Great prices! Everything must go!" They rolled up, they rolled up, hands reaching out, money flying, suits swishing off the table.

It was over in minutes.

"Roll up, roll up!" I shouted, ringing the big brass bell, like Father Christmas. "Big sale today! Don't miss out! Great prices! Everything must go!" They rolled up, they rolled up, hands reaching out, money flying back and forth, suits swishing off the table.

Inside the store, I counted the notes and coins. One fifty, three, seven fifty, twelve… twenty-two! I'd made R22! Enough for the roller skates—and then some.

I stashed the money in an old butter dish, holding it tightly when I returned with my grandparents to the supermarket. I wasn't excited; I was petrified. What if some other kid had bought the skates? I ran to the sports section. I scanned the shelves. And there they were. I picked them up and hugged them. I felt like a superhero, a warrior, a princess, a movie star. I was Marilyn, on roller skates!

On the pathway of my grandparents' home, I unwrapped the skates, put them on my feet, laced them up, and stood proud, tall, and a little unsteady. I looked down at my pretty pink roller skates, with the black velvet trimming. I bent down, slowly, and took them off. I put them away in a cupboard at home, and I never wore them again.

Why?

Because I realized, as soon as I saw them on my feet, that I had never really wanted them in the first place. I'd had a dream, a fantasy, an unattainable goal.

And I had just wanted my dream to come true.

Even today, living in a world so different from the one I once knew—the world of startups and investing and entrepreneurship in Silicon Valley—I still remember those pretty pink roller skates, and the lesson they taught me.

> *Even today, living in a world so different from the one I knew, I still think of those pretty pink roller skates, and I still remember the lesson they taught me.*

There are always dreams to be chased, and there are always ways to catch them. And even when you *do* grab hold of them, further down the road, there are bigger and better dreams, daring you to make them come true. All you have to do is click your heels, like Dorothy in *The Wizard of Oz*.

Come, join me now on my journey, and let me show you the way.

Find Your Superpower

At the tender age of five, I got my first—and last—workplace demotion. My mom moved me from the front of the store, where I had been happily greeting customers, to the back, where I was appointed a "floor manager." It was a *sweeping* change. I was pleased to be handed the authority to wield the ancient broom, with its stiff bristles that did little more than shift the dirt around. But I missed smiling and chatting with people as they walked in from the street. Ah, well. I was just a kid, and it did make a nice change from my daytime hours at school.

I had just graduated from kindergarten and had been granted a scholarship to Carmel, an upscale Jewish school. Most would view this as a positive move, but even then, I knew I had three strikes against me. The first being that I didn't know a single classmate going in. The other students had spent kindergarten together the year before, establishing a hierarchy of their own.

When I walked into Carmel with my Audrey Hepburn haircut, a safety-pinned dress, and a toothy smile, I was not well-received. Strike two, I guessed, came from the whispers of parents and teachers.

My family wasn't wealthy, and my father was 27 years older than my mother. Most importantly, the school was Orthodox Jewish. You would think my father being Orthodox and my mother converting to Judaism years before would've been my qualifier. Unfortunately, most converted Jews are considered Reform when they convert. My mother being Reform meant that I was Reform and therefore "different." The third strike came from home. Granny, my mother's mother, was anti-Semitic. She went to great lengths to show it. She drove 40 miles to the store almost every day, finding new and creative ways to insult my school and the life we were living. If my own grandmother didn't like me, how were the kids at school ever going to accept me?

"The only way you'll survive in this environment is to win," my mother told me, matter-of-fact. "You have to be the best. Always be the best."

Straight A's were the *only* acceptable grade. So, I got straight A's. From my grandmother's disapproval to my mother's expectations, I had little time to wonder what I would like to do with my life. Instead, I was *told*: I loved music, and lived to play the violin.

But when my mother took me to see Mr. Sack, the music teacher, and I lifted my hand-me-down instrument from its case, he stopped me cold and said he wanted to first look at my hands. He felt my finger pads and nodded to himself, like a doctor about to deliver a serious diagnosis. He turned to my mother and said, "She's a cellist."

> *He felt my finger pads and nodded to himself, like a doctor about to deliver a serious diagnosis. He turned to my mother and said, "She's a cellist."*

I hated the hefty instrument, with its curvy hips, its girdled waist, its end-pin *jabbing* at the floor, like a ballerina frozen *en pointe*. To me, a cello was to a violin like a bumblebee to a butterfly.

But then I learned to play it. And Mr. Sack, as it turned out, was right. He was a cellist himself, and he could sense in me a kindred spirit, just by reading my palms. To my mother's delight, after just a few lessons, Mr. Sack said I was naturally talented, and that I would one day play on the great stages of the world.

I was less delighted by the prospect.

Already, I was the weird kid in school, an easy target for bullying by the Mean Girls who lived in their mansions on the hill. And now I was the weird kid with the *cello*, the uncoolest of uncool instruments, hauling it around in a conspicuous, torso-shaped case that was taller than me, going off to practice at Mr. Sack's for hours and hours each day.

But the playing came easy.

As I worked my way through the standard repertoire—the Top Ten Hits of the Classical Cello—I felt like I was teasing the strings with every fiber of my being, rather than the stretched-taut strings of a heartwood bow.

One day, Mr. Sack said he had something to give me, a special delivery, all the way from London. I opened the envelope with trembling hands. It was a brand-new manuscript of the music for a piece by Gabriel Fauré: *Apres un Reve*. After a dream. I was stunned. All the other manuscripts were old and tattered. This one fresh, pristine, untouched by anyone—besides me. It was one of the few new things I had ever owned.

I played the notes with pride and love, striving for perfection, blistering my fingers in the intensity of the pursuit. Mr. Sack was angry about that. I had crossed the line. I was trying too hard, playing to *impress* myself, losing the vital connection between me and the instrument. He steered me away from the architecture of the music, all the way back to the building blocks: the beginner's set.

He made me play the same bar, over and over, all the while filling my head with visions of the path that lay ahead: to the Royal Academy of Music in London, to the stages of Europe, to the *world*.

But all I could think of was the ultimate reward that lay waiting for me. Not the applause, not the acclaim, not the bouquets of fresh flowers in my calloused hands.

All I wanted was a Big Mac and Fries from the McDonald's up the road, my incentive from mother for carrying on practicing. And practicing. And practicing.

Playing was easy. Practicing was hard.

But my mother had decided I was to give up ordinary school and become a full-time cellist. I would practice for eight hours a day, with interludes of meditation to ease my string-tight nerves. I would record an album which would be sent to all the major labels. I would embark on a concert tour, as the next Yo-Yo Ma, the next Vanessa Mae, the first great *maestra* of the cello, all the way from the edge-pin of the African continent.

But that's the trouble with other people's dreams. They're *other* people's dreams. I had different plans in mind. I wanted to be the *maestra* of my own destiny.

> *That's the trouble with other people's dreams. They're other people's dreams. I had different plans in mind. I wanted to be the maestra of my own destiny.*

"She'll enjoy it eventually," Mr. Sack would tell my mother. "It's her destiny. Why else would she be so good?" That was the common belief of almost everyone around me. They were convinced that my uncertainty, my dislike of the cello, would fade with age. What I couldn't articulate back then has since become the guiding principle of my life. The principle that everyone has their own unique superpower. A job, a skill, or an art form that they are especially qualified to offer the world.

I knew my superpower wasn't playing the cello. It would take me a while to be able to define what it was, but I felt the first stirrings on the day my parents took me for an outing, to a big wholesale store called Jumbo Cash & Carry.

As we walked across the parking lot, I saw people carrying boxes of super-size Omo, South Africa's number 1 selling laundry powder. They were the biggest boxes I'd ever seen. At the entrance to the store was a fuzzy pink mass. As we got closer, I could see it was made up of thousands of bottles of pink lotion, stacked on wooden crates and secured by plastic wrap. My heart started racing. I didn't know why.

I walked with my parents past row after row of stock, smiling at each person who went by. Even at six years old, I knew what this business meant.

The owners of Jumbo Cash & Carry were immigrants, just like my family. Queues of people surrounded us, tallying orders on calculators, and fanning out wads of notes as they got to the front of the line. You could spend up to R500 on an order, and they were strict about it. I counted the queue in front of us. There were 10 tellers, with an average of 10 people in each line. I thought that was long, until I wandered off to the other side, where there were 26 tellers tending to orders.

I knew there was a big difference between Jumbo Cash & Carry and my father's business, but I wouldn't be able to define what it was until much later. For now, all I wanted was to be in business myself. I absorbed every piece of information I could. Chatty kid that I was, I made friends with the bossman. "Where are all those crates of pink lotion going?" I asked. "They're going to Africa," he smiled. Africa! We were in South Africa, but the rest of the continent was a mystery to me. I wandered down the aisles, like an explorer on a trek to faraway lands.

I saw rows of jewelry cases, make-up bags, hair accessories, belts, and boxes of nail polish, stacked three stories high. I rounded a corner and my eyes widened. Perfume! I sprayed some on my wrist, testing one scent, then the next. I felt giddy with delight. In years to come, I would turn that feeling—that sweet smell of success—into an equation for aspiring entrepreneurs.

Superpower = something you're good at and obsessed with + a way to make money from it

My visit to Jumbo Cash & Carry that Sunday was the first time I had used the equation on myself. At school the next day, I asked my classmates about their stationery, pencil cases, key rings, hair accessories, and so on—what they wanted, what they needed, and most importantly, what they'd pay. Based on that research, I returned to Jumbo and did the math. There were plenty of products I could buy—and then *sell,* for a tidy profit.

I ran the idea by my older brother. He leaped on board and we were in business!

> *Superpower = something you're good at and obsessed with + a way to make money from it.*

The next Sunday, we took our small cut of earnings from the shop and bought products based on the interests of my classmates. We brought our stock home, set the pricing, and projected our profitability. My brother was kind enough to give me a small float, knowing I would need change for our customers. I borrowed a red plastic vanity case from my granny to carry my stock, and a notebook to record sales.

When I clicked open that vanity case, something powerful happened. The kids who had excluded me, who'd made me feel different and less than, were suddenly buying my products. I had something they wanted. I had a place in their ecosystem. They were my customers.

I sold out on day one. Every Sunday, my brother and I would buy more stock at Jumbo Cash & Carry. I quickly learned what sold and what didn't. Nail polish, in bright colors, sold fast. We bought a pack of 10 for R4.99, and sold each bottle for R4.99, a nice profit for a couple of kids. What didn't sell were the Gothic colors—the black and the deep purple. I had a dark idea.

We took the leftover bottles of nail polish to the shop, where they fitted in perfectly with the vampire costumes. They were an instant hit. Like Dracula, we wanted to get our teeth stuck in, so we looked around for other opportunities.

We tried selling stock at Pro Arte, the music school where I played cello. But unlike my private school, which was filled with children from wealthy families, the kids at Pro Arte had earned their place through merit, rather than money. They didn't have the disposable income needed to support our business. Lesson learned: stick to your target market. But after three years in business, my classmates were changing too. They were becoming more sophisticated. They wanted LA Gear and Nintendo Game Boys, strobe lights and laser pointers.

The best I could offer in the electronics department were no-name boomboxes with terrible sound quality. Even if I could sell them at a profit, how was I going to carry boomboxes to and from school? Where was I going to store them? We lived in a dangerous part of Johannesburg and were robbed often.

I realized that our entrepreneurial endeavor was missing a key ingredient for long-term success. Scalability. Still, I had discovered my superpower—the ability to recognize a great entrepreneurial endeavor. To this day, I get great joy from assessing startups, picking founders, and investing in a vision. It would take me years to harness my superpower and turn it into something scalable, but even as a child, I saw opportunities in the most unlikely places.

I realized that our entrepreneurial endeavor was missing a key ingredient for long-term success. Scalability. Still, I had discovered my superpower —the ability to recognize a great entrepreneurial endeavor.

We lived in Johannesburg, or Joburg as we called it. My school and the shop were 40 miles away, in Pretoria. Every day, we commuted, and every day I stared out the window in awe. I knew exactly what I was looking at, but no one else in the car could see it. I was looking at opportunity.

For miles and miles, there was nothing out there but wide-open land. The only structure that stood out was a shed, with a wooden sign reading, "Fruit for Sale," in white chalk. It was like a scene from one of my father's beloved Western movies. The frontier lay waiting.

One day, the words on the wooden sign changed. "Land for Sale," it read. "Look," I shouted, "Land! We have to buy!" Everyone in the car laughed. But I was serious. I knew that land was the most precious commodity. And I knew that this stretch, between two major cities, was ripe for development. If thousands of people were making the journey back and forth every day, wouldn't it make sense for them to move somewhere in the middle? "Fine," I said. "I'll buy it myself."

One day soon after, I walked into Standard Bank, carrying a bag of cash. I was a regular, entrusted to deposit the daily takings from my dad's shop. The tellers knew me well. I was sure they would understand my plan. "Hello," I said, standing on tiptoe at the counter.

"I need a loan to buy a big piece of land. It's between Johannesburg and Pretoria." Again, the sound of grown-ups laughing.

I was nine years old. I was furious. Why wouldn't they listen to me? I didn't get my loan, but I did learn two important lessons.

One: Have the courage, confidence, and patience to believe in yourself. The bank was not the first nor the last naysayer I would encounter in my career. No one was going to hand me opportunities on a platter. If I truly believed in something, nothing would be able to stop me. Not my age, my gender, or my financial situation. I had to be the first person to invest in my dreams.

And two: I was right!

I can't blame the bank for not giving a loan to a nine-year-old. But that doesn't change the fact that I saw an opportunity, and I knew with all my heart that something would come of it. As it turned out, someone did buy my beloved piece of land. It's now called the

Midrand Corridor, and it's one of the most valuable stretches of property in all of South Africa.

Bigger dreams would come my way, and one day, I would fulfill them.

But first came the nightmares.

And they were even more real.

THREE

Find the Power in Your Pain

I held my breath each time we opened our front door. Coming home was like pulling the lever on a slot machine. Most days, we would find the place just as we left it. But every so often, we'd stumble on the familiar mess of a robbery. Drawers pulled open, valuables gone, sundry possessions scattered on the floor. We felt violated, but somehow lucky.

All 12 of the "successful" break-ins at our house happened in broad daylight when we were not home. And that's not counting the regular thefts from our clothesline and our cars, or the interrupted attempts made in the middle of the night.

I can't recall how many times we were woken up by the sound of an intruder scaling our fence. Thankfully, in each instance, we were able to call the cops in time. Friends, neighbors, and even my grandparents weren't as lucky.

My granny was beaten to within an inch of her life during a break-in one Sunday afternoon. The robber stole her jewelry and left her for dead. My father and I rushed over with the police, but every night I was afraid the man would come back.

These crimes were terrible, and we lived in constant fear. But they were a product, too, of a cruel and inhuman system that governed and divided the lives of every South African.

In the 1980s, apartheid was at its peak, with the ruling party entrenching its power through a series of states of emergency. There was a blackout on news, but the sirens and helicopters told us all we needed to know. Just a short drive from where we lived, people were being shot, rounded up, and brutalized.

Our suburb, designated by law for whites only, was on the boundary of Alexandra, one of the poorest black neighborhoods in the country. Informally known as "Gomora," after the city destroyed by vengeful fire in the Book of Genesis, Alexandra was a sprawling, haphazard township where more than 170,000 people lived in poverty. The inequality was grueling, and it drove many to a life of crime.

My family and I were of Jewish refugee stock. We had little to our name. But we were white according to the law, and that was the passport to a life of relative ease and privilege. Joe's Pharmacy, my father's combination drugstore and costume hire store, was situated directly across from the central police station in Pretoria, the seat of the South African government. All around us were government buildings, gray and austere in the brutalist architectural style, symbolizing the might of the apartheid state.

> *In the 1980s, apartheid was at its peak, with the ruling party entrenching its power through a series of states of emergency. There was a blackout on news, but the police sirens and the thunder of helicopters told us all we needed to know.*

Many of our customers, classified by law as Black, Colored, or Indian, were government employees who didn't have access to medical care. For some, my father's pharmacy was the only option because he refused to charge them. The government employees spent their days serving a system that denied them basic human rights. The black police officers put their lives on the line every day, defending a system that oppressed them. My father's kindness was a small gesture in the grand scheme of things, but the people we helped went on to return the favor when we needed them most.

It was late on a Wednesday night, and my father still hadn't come home from the shop. We sat at home, the clock tick-tick-ticking. It was unusual for my father to be out this late, with no earlier contact to let us know where he was.

We called the police. They told us we would only be able to file a missing person's report once 24 hours had gone by. We painfully waited until Thursday night and submitted the report as soon as we could.

At 5 pm on Friday, the telephone rang. The police had found my father in the intensive care ward at a hospital. He had been in a car crash on Wednesday night. My mother and brother rushed to the hospital. They were too late.

After 12 hours on the operating table, my father had been declared brain-dead and the neurosurgeon had turned off his life support.

Joe, the kindest man I had ever known, my father, my inspiration, the source of my "divine sparkle," was gone. That Sunday, in accordance with Jewish law, he was buried. So loved and admired was he that his funeral was the second-largest in the history of Pretoria. We were surrounded by masses of people, crying.

Men from the Orthodox community took my brother into a room for Kriah, a Jewish tradition of tearing one's shirt to express grief. We went through the motions, but it was all so overwhelming.

I stood and watched the mourners shoveling soil onto my father's grave. Everything felt strange and unstable. I was angry with my father for leaving me alone. I felt guilty, and I still do, for not being able to take better care of him.

But the strangest thing of all was my mother's reaction.

"Do not tell anyone your father died," she warned me, on the way to school the next day. "They will treat you like a victim and a charity case." She believed success was built on strength, not vulnerability. Then she gave me my instructions. "Your job is to lead our family out of darkness and into the light, like Moses leading the Jews out of Egypt," she said. A lot to ask of a 10-year-old, but I nodded my head and held the tears at bay.

My mother was an enigma. To the world, she was a perfect

lady, quiet, demure, unassuming. But below the surface lay a fury and anger that was only shown to a select few. My father had been one of them.

I had been another.

I always felt that my mother hated me. She threatened to send me to an orphanage, fueling my extreme anxiety as a child. On the rare occasion that she was kind enough to feed us dinner as a family, and I asked what she was cooking, her response would be: "Poison." I had seen the way she treated and belittled my father. I was scared of her rage. Without his protection, I knew she would need to find another target.

"Your job is to lead our family out of darkness and into the light, like Moses leading the Jews out of Egypt," she said. It was a lot to ask of a 10-year-old, but I nodded my head and held the tears at bay.

I grew used to her temper, which quickly spun out of control and turned into physical abuse. She would hit me, slap me, pull my hair, dig her fingernails into my arm. For days, I would carry the bruises. And so many years later, deep inside me, I still carry the scars.

I always felt that my only salvation was through excelling and helping the family, but it was never enough.

It also pained me to see my brother, Richard, cast aside, as if he didn't matter. Intellectually, he was exceptional, a natural-born entrepreneur. But in the family dynamic, he was the black sheep, nicknamed "Dick" and treated with disdain, for reasons I could never fathom. It hurt me even more when my mother turned him against me, weaponizing my own brother in her relentless and inexplicable war against me.

Sometimes, it is the people closest to you who can cause the greatest damage to your self-worth.

I didn't tell a single person my dad had died until I was 21. We never visited his grave. There was no time to grieve. It wasn't long before my father's absence presented a whole new set of problems, beyond the emotional toll.

The financial records of Joe's Pharmacy were turned over to my mother. It soon became clear that money management had not been my father's superpower. I still believe he did the right thing by providing free medicine to those in need. But I wish there was something we could have done to offset the cost while he was still alive. The bills began to pile up.

We owed money to the water and power department, pharmaceutical wholesalers, and most importantly, the bank. Our home mortgage hadn't been paid in years. The shop had taken out multiple business loans, dating back decades. We were drowning in debt.

We still had the business, but it was an eccentric hybrid—a combination drugstore and costume rental store. My dad was the only pharmacist in our family, so all we had were the costumes. My mother, brother, and I had to destroy bags of costly medication, which we couldn't legally sell or even give away.

It felt like we were destroying my dad's legacy of hard work, kindness, and dedication. The costumes were old, tired, and in need of a serious upgrade. There was no money to make it happen.

I lived on adrenaline, trying to make good with what we had. But I knew it wasn't going to be enough to save us.

We worked at the shop until midnight, trying to find a way to make money with no money. Some nights, we didn't even go home. I would lay the fuzzy gorilla suit on the floor, under the costume rails, just to get a couple of hours of sleep. With all the break-ins at home, it felt safer in the shop. But that feeling didn't last.

> *We worked at the shop until midnight, trying to find a way to make money with no money. Some nights, we didn't even go home. I would lay the fuzzy gorilla suit on the floor, under the costume rails, just to get a couple of hours of sleep.*

One night, there was a drunken brawl just outside. I was used to the screaming and the gunshots, so it didn't wake me at first. That was until one guy threw the other guy through our storefront window. The shattering glass woke me up instantly. Not just to what was happening, but to the reality of my life. I was just a kid, in way over my head. I was 10. I wasn't Moses, leading the Jews out of slavery, no matter what my mother may have told me.

My father's death, my mother's abusive tendencies, our financial uncertainty, compounded the pressure I felt. Instead of buckling at my knees, I harnessed that energy into an insatiable drive. I wasn't the only one. My brother must have had the same reaction. One day, he had an epiphany.

He decided to write to embassies, requesting lists of suppliers overseas. The catalogs arrived. We picked out the stock we liked. Highly coveted merchandise from America, England, and France. We could only afford the shipping costs, so we had to sell the free samples.

My brother and I showed the stock around school. More people started coming to the shop. Even with our increased profit margin, our cash was limited. We weren't making enough to pay debts and order more stock. We kept on requesting new samples. We knew the suppliers would eventually catch on to our ruse. We needed a new plan.

My mother's words rang in my ears. "Your job is to lead our family out of darkness and into the light." I needed a way to make money that didn't rely on stock. My best bet was to tap again into the disposable income of my classmates. But how? My customers were losing interest in our small range of products. My new endeavor would have to be based on service. And the best service I could supply was my intellect.

As the top student in my class, I had a powerful tool at my disposal. Leverage. I began tutoring my peers. They got results. The more kids I helped, the more their parents were willing to pay for my guidance. I was particularly gifted in everyone's trickiest subject, Afrikaans. That was my niche.

Word spread, and I even wound up tutoring Nelson Mandela's grandson. I was always amazed that a kid from such an auspicious family could be so incredibly well-behaved and brought up. I zeroed in on the wealthiest, most high-profile kids. My reputation grew. Some of my clients liked me enough to bring me souvenirs from their holidays at the Olympics and five-star ski resorts in Switzerland.

My brother followed my lead and started tutoring too. We managed to stay afloat, but still didn't have enough to pay down the debts. We were running to stand still. The samples kept coming in from our suppliers, but we had to concoct ever more elaborate stories as to why we needed so many. Our system was heading for collapse. There had to be another way.

We needed credit, and that meant we had to take a trip overseas. My brother stayed behind to run the shop, while my mother and I traveled to the UK to meet with suppliers. We were desperate to import anything, but the quality had to be decent. Meeting suppliers in person would reassure them that our business was legitimate, and would prove to us that the products were worth the money.

Catalogs had fooled us in the past. We had seen a growing demand for women's wigs, and thought we'd make a killing selling them to salons. We found a supplier. The catalogs showed images of beautiful, silky hair, modeled by happy-looking women. The prices were good, too. But when the wigs arrived, the hair was harsh and coarse. I could barely run my hand through the strands.

Instead of the black and brown colors we had ordered, each wig was peroxide blonde. Who was going to want to look like a dime-store version of Marilyn Monroe? Pictures can be deceiving. And so can people.

> *When the wigs arrived, the hair was harsh and coarse to the touch. Instead of the black and brown colors we had ordered, each wig was peroxide blonde. Who was going to want to look like a dime-store version of Marilyn Monroe?*

When we arrived in the UK, a nice man picked us up in a minivan. He drove us straight to a factory two hours away. I was still sick from the plane, where I had thrown up my breakfast. The man chatted away while I stared out the window. Everything seemed foreign until we passed a BP gas station. The sight of something familiar calmed me. I may have been a foreigner in this place, but that didn't matter. We were there for something bigger than country borders or language barriers. We were there for business.

I shook off the motion sickness as we pulled up to the factory.

They had every type of costume accessory, from plastic swords, to fireman's helmets, to clip-on cat tails. I walked around with the owners, asking about the product ranges, their costs, and availability. If the suppliers thought I was too young to be asking such questions, they didn't show it.

The paperwork was turned over to my mother, and they agreed to give us limited quantities, with the ability to size up our orders, contingent on our capacity to make good. The UK suppliers were just the beginning. As soon as we were able to secure a line of credit and generate revenue, we had the cash we needed to look elsewhere.

Some of my classmates were embassy kids from the U.S. and Canada. They hosted dress-up parties for Independence Day, St. Patrick's Day, and Halloween. We were happy to be their costume supplier of choice. I sat next to George Lo and Rachel Wong in class. They were smart immigrant kids from wealthy families. I got to know them well. They told me stories about their lives, their culture, and the growing economy in Hong Kong.

I told my brother. He contacted the embassy and got a list of suppliers in Hong Kong. We were put in touch with a man named Nigel Farmer. His wife was native to China, but lived in Hong Kong. Mr. and Mrs. Farmer agreed to work with us on the same credit terms as the factories in the UK.

My mother and I began planning a trip, but the cost was prohibitive. To spend a large amount of money traveling and come back with nothing was a gamble. We knew if we were going to make the journey, we had to make good use of our time.

After careful research, we added more stops to the itinerary. In *Time*, I read about the rise of Singapore as an economic superpower. My brother contacted the Singapore embassy for a list of suppliers. Thailand wasn't yet widely known for low-cost goods, but we heard whispers and added Bangkok to the list. After securing multiple deals, we felt comfortable enough to order big containers of stock. Considering where we started, this was a huge accomplishment.

We began supplying event planners with decorations and other goods, alongside our tried and trusted costumes. Did we work hard? Yes, but there was a bigger secret to our success. Many of our wholesalers, especially in Asia, were family-run businesses. They admired us for keeping our father's shop open, and his dream alive.

We didn't have boundless financial assets or a legacy of rich entrepreneurial endeavor, but we had fond memories of the man who raised and inspired us, and his reputation became our calling-card.

We shared newspaper clippings and photographs of my father Joe, Hollywood stylist, posing with the famous stars of the day. We told the story of how he and his family had fled Lithuania by boat in 1929, docking in South Africa with only the clothes on their backs.

How he had opened a pharmacy at the age of 28, but had yearned for something different, something bigger, something to equal his other great passion in life — the performing arts. How he had left his deputy in charge of the pharmacy, and had gone to work in the theater business, under Max Factor, the cosmetics icon.

It was a riveting story, glittering with the dazzle of showbiz, but anchored in the grit of a hardscrabble life. It was as if our dad was still with us, as we introduced our credentials a world away from our own. The ties of family connected us to complete strangers who became business partners.

People from all walks of life loved and respected my father. Our shop, which is still open for business, holds a great deal of goodwill due to his reputation. It's run by my brother, Richard, and my mother, and it's now called Joe's Magical Party Hire.

Many of our wholesalers, especially in Asia, were family-run businesses. They admired us for keeping our father's shop open, and his dream alive.

In my dreams I still wander through the racks of costumes, and I see my father, smiling his dazzling smile as he leads his customers by the arm. But in all these years, I've never gone back to the shop to see for myself. It holds too many memories, and the bad overshadow the good.

As for my mother, the gulf between us has only widened. She wanted me to be Moses, leading my family into the light. Instead, all that happened is that the sea parted, with her on one side of the world and me on the other.

The last time I saw my mother, by chance, was at a high-profile business event in Johannesburg. During the keynote, I slipped out to freshen up. There were two people in the restroom—my mother and I. Our eyes locked in the mirror, but she didn't even acknowledge my existence. I walked out, devastated. A dozen years had passed since we had last been in each other's presence.

I had an epiphany that our entire relationship had been built on my achievements. She had raised the bar so high that it became harder and harder for me to deliver. Nothing I could ever do was enough.

It has taken me two decades to realize that I can't live for other people. That I need to prioritize my own needs over the needs of others.

What caused me the most pain in that moment in the restroom, was that my existence was not validated or even recognized by my own mother. I may as well have been born in a test tube. It was a deeply strange feeling that haunted me for years.

Only very recently have I been able to fill that void myself, with self-healing and self-love.

Only very recently have I been able to realize the truth—that I am who I am, and that who I am…is enough.

There were two people in the restroom—my mother and I. She didn't even acknowledge my existence. I walked out, devastated.

FOUR

Leverage the Positive Power of Compound Interest

I like to think of myself as a positive person. More so, that's what I choose to be. My life has been a journey across peaks and valleys, good roads and bad. While I appreciate the good times, I also recognize the lasting impact and potential value of the bad. Sometimes, the worst experiences can mold and shape us for the better.

Take my lifestyle, for example. I exercise, do yoga, meditate daily, and follow a strict and healthy diet. At the same time, my disciplines and rituals of self-care are actually a mechanism for survival, a way of overcoming the legacy of my mother's abuse. She made me think of myself as unlovable and repulsive. I am still plagued by nightmares and insomnia as a result.

But when we survive a waking, living nightmare, when we are driven down by a sudden and brutal act of violence—as I was on that terrible night of the carjacking outside our home—it can steel our resolve to rise again. A bullet has the power to draw blood and shatter bone. But it can't stand in the way of a dream.

You were lucky.

That's what we used to say in my old home city of Johannesburg, as a way of consoling someone who had been a victim of a crime, but had somehow, miraculously, made it out alive. "It could have been worse," we say, as if pain and trauma can be measured on a sliding scale.

We could never breathe easy in our place of birth. We loved South Africa, but living on the edge, in constant fear of crime and violence, was taking its toll. No matter how much security we had in place—alarms, panic buttons, cameras, high walls crowned with razor-wire, armed responders on constant patrol—we never felt safe from possible harm.

But there was more to it than that.

My relationship with my mother had reached its lowest ebb. She would tell me, every day, that she loved me less than the day before, and that the day would come when she would not love me at all. I don't know, looking back, if she had ever really loved me.

At the age of 15, I was naive enough to believe that things would get better if we left South Africa for another country. I knew so many people who had taken that route, to travel, to study, to work, to *escape*. I thought of my uncle, a medical doctor, who had made a new start in a harbor city called St. John's, in an island province whose very name resonated with the clarion call of opportunity. Newfoundland.

He would call my mother once a week, to tell her about the joys of life in his new home. Canada, he said, was peaceful, equitable, and hospitable, especially to South Africans. His children, my cousins, were thriving in their new environment. While their biggest challenge was learning French, mine was recovering from a gunshot wound.

"We have to leave!" I screamed at my mother. In an uncharacteristically rational moment, she heard me and agreed. She knew that fleeing was our only option.

Once I was patched up, I went back to school, but my mind was fixated on Canada. As luck would have it, the Canadian Ambassador's daughter, Maya, was a close friend of mine. I flooded her with questions, wanting to learn anything and everything about her homeland. Her family hosted dress-up parties at the Embassy. They would come to the shop for supplies.

One day, a member of the Embassy staff told me about a new immigration program in the Atlantic Provinces of Canada. My eyes lit up. I began plotting our escape.

I learned there was a busy film industry in Nova Scotia, a maritime province surrounded by rolling seas and lush forests. Maybe we could manufacture costumes in South Africa, and supply them at a competitive cost to movie production companies. That would make us eligible for Canadian government sponsorship. My brother conducted research online. "Look," he said, "I've found the perfect spot."

He showed me a picture of a sailing boat in an idyllic coastal setting. A seaport called Halifax. That's how our dream began: two kids at the foot of Africa, looking at a pretty picture of a boat on the other side of the world. There was a catch, of course. The weather in Halifax was cold and wet, with snow for 69 days of the year. It was the opposite of our mild and sunny climate in Johannesburg. But we needed a change.

The weather in Halifax was cold and wet, with snow for 69 days of the year. It was the opposite of our mild and sunny climate in Johannesburg. But we needed a change.

There were three steps to the visa application, the first being the paperwork. We were used to it, keeping track of stock, making timely payments to suppliers, and maintaining financial records for our shop. But it was nothing compared to the deluge of visa forms and record requests. Most people hire an immigration lawyer. We couldn't afford that luxury. We did it ourselves. Next came the medical exams.

Apparently, living on adrenaline takes a toll on the human body. My heart was beating so fast that the immigration doctors thought I had a cardiac problem. It took me three attempts to convince them I was just nervous.

The third and final step was the interviews. My mother and I met with the Trade Department in Halifax. The team noted my Audrey Hepburn haircut, and I smiled and warmed up quickly. I spoke of my entrepreneurial vision and what we could do for Canada. We made it through.

The next interview took place at the Canadian Embassy in London. I felt a weight lifted from my shoulders as the confirmation came. We were formally granted permanent resident status. Canada was exactly as my uncle had described. I felt safe. I felt free. I had the gift of opportunities I could only have dreamed of back home. Still, I wasn't prepared for the weather. We were staying at the YMCA in Halifax. It was winter.

Back home in Joburg, winter was a mild and sunny season, with a light dusting of snow every few years. Here, I finally understood what it means to be cold. Every morning, on the way to school, I would hide from the wind in the doorway of the nearest building. When the traffic light turned green, I would sprint from block to block, doing my best to keep warm.

My brother was still in South Africa, wrapping up the business. I thrived at school, becoming the top student in my class. But if the weather in Nova Scotia was different, so was the education system. I was in Grade 12, my final year. To graduate, I needed to complete a Grade 9 class on "Career and Life Management." We had no such thing in South Africa. But the principles I learned on the course would change my life forever. The most radical was a principle that Albert Einstein called the "eighth wonder of the world." Compound interest.

Let's say I have $200 sitting in an account with an interest rate of 5%. After the first year, the 5% interest will turn that $200 into $210. In the second year, the 5% will be applied on $210, equaling $220.50. If you leave that $200 to collect 5% annual interest, you will double your investment in less than 15 years. Now $400 is a small amount in the grand scheme of things, but imagine what you could earn with a bigger investment.

> *The principles I learned in the course would change my life forever. And the most radical of them all was a principle that Albert Einstein called the "eighth wonder of the world." Compound interest.*

When my "Career and Life Management" teacher explained the principle to our class, I was immediately reminded of my grandfather. His name was Neville Clifton, and he was an engineering professor. He didn't earn much, but he was cautious with money. In contrast, his wife, Gwenda, my granny, was an aspiring socialite. She could never understand why her husband would lock himself in the back room of their house. What was he doing in there? Well, it turns out he was making a fortune.

After he died from a heart attack, my granny went through his will and found four ruled pages detailing his investments in over 120 listed companies. He had harnessed his mathematical abilities, making small investments over time. These grew into substantial stock in some of the world's top companies. Compounding was my grandfather's superpower.

My granny was overjoyed. No longer would she have to live a frugal lifestyle, watching every penny. For the next 50 years, she lived it up like her role model, The Queen of England. When she wanted to take a luxury holiday or buy new designer clothes, she would sell shares. By the time my granny died, all the money was gone.

I could have been upset, like the rest of my family, that granny had blown through the inheritance we desperately needed. But I wasn't. Instead, I was inspired by my grandfather. He had proved to be a wise and farsighted investor. Maybe I could learn to be one too.

My granny and grandfather epitomized the paradox of money versus wealth. Norman Clifton used what little disposable income he had to amass great wealth. He could have lived out his retirement years comfortably, but he died fairly young.

My granny liquidated their stock without much concern for longevity. I often wonder what value those stocks would hold today. I wish my grandfather had enjoyed his wealth while he was alive, instead of leaving it to be squandered by his sole beneficiary.

Contrary to popular belief, money is not the root of all evil. It is the common denominator we use to accumulate wealth. Having spent a good portion of my life without money, I'd be lying if I said it didn't make things easier. Money satisfies our needs, but never fulfills our dreams.

Without preparation, education, and leverage, money will never turn into true wealth. To identify these tenets of wealth creation, I had to find an example of what true wealth looked like. I found it very close to home.

My uncle had become a successful doctor by the time we made it to Canada. He found medicine rewarding, but a doctor can only book so many appointments in a day. From a business perspective, his work lacked leverage. My uncle could have followed in the footsteps of my grandfather, investing part of his income and enjoying the benefits of compound interest. But he had another idea.

He leveraged his experience in medicine to become CEO of one of the biggest drug companies in the world. He worked hard, but most of his success was due to his foresight.

My mother and I would occasionally go to dinner with my uncle and his family. He would insist we order multiple courses and expensive wines. I spent most of my meal worrying about how we'd pay for it. At the end of the evening, he wouldn't even look at the bill. He would hand his Platinum American Express card to the waiter, and it would be taken care of. That's what wealth looks like, I thought to myself.

I graduated from high school as the top student in the Province of Nova Scotia. At the ceremony, I gave the commencement address for my class and was awarded by the Governor-General. I received a full University scholarship and was set to graduate with honors. A bright future lay ahead for me.

But my mother had other plans.

She had always been hesitant about our big move. I thought our newfound success and safety would prove to her that the change was not only necessary, but positive for us all. I was wrong. She couldn't cope with change. Every few months, she'd come up with some excuse or threat as to why we needed to return to South Africa. I assumed this was a natural adjustment period and her fears would dissipate over time. I was wrong again.

One evening, my mother told us she had given up our immigration papers. We were going to be deported. She was lying, but how were we to know? I was 18 and a valedictorian. I could have pushed back. I could have fought against her abuse and self-destruction. But after all these years, I felt drained. Leaving Canada broke my heart, but not my spirit. I had caught a glimpse of the life that I wanted to live, if I could only get away again.

It took me years to realize why my mother chose violence and financial ruin over positive change. She used the power of compounding too, but in a negative sense. Just as interest increases the value of an investment and in turn increases the amount of interest, she had built up her despair over time. Back in South Africa, her abuse followed the same pattern. I began to fear for my life.

I still feel sorry for my mother. She was unable to enjoy the opportunities we found in Canada. There was nothing I could do to change her mind. The only future I had any control over was my own. Today, I guide aspiring entrepreneurs and CEOs, many of them already world-class professionals, through the fundamentals of wealth creation. There are three principles that separate the truly wealthy from the average person.

1. Education. This doesn't need to be "formal," but it should be extensive in a chosen area of expertise.
2. Desire. Be clear on what you want, and why you want it.
3. Commitment. You are always the first person to invest in your idea. Develop the endurance needed to achieve your goals, even if it takes decades.

My experience in Canada taught me that the people you surround yourself with have a greater effect on your success than you might think. There was one good thing that came from going back home. I was able to put that theory to the test, when I met a man who would change my life for the better.

> *It took me years to realize why my mother did all of this, why she would rather choose the prospect of violence and financial despair over positive change. My mother compounded on a negative outlook.*

FIVE

Dare to Share What You Know

Back home in Johannesburg, the city I thought I had left behind for good, I was working out one morning at my local Virgin Active gym. But I wasn't running on the treadmill. I wasn't lifting weights. I was exercising my mind. I had completed my Bachelor's Degree in Statistics and Actuarial Science before we left Canada, and was now preparing for my board exams. I spent a lot of my study time on a public computer at the gym, which was part of Richard Branson's global business empire.

I liked being in a place that distilled the essence of his entrepreneurial energy. The buzz of people working out on the equipment and in the pool added to the air of positive endeavor. I had a network of like-minded people around me, and I enjoyed the reprieve from the stress and chaos of my mother's home. But as I sat there staring at the spreadsheet on the screen, I was stumped.

I was working on a particularly difficult financial swap calculation, and I couldn't figure out the answer. I looked at the studious young man sitting at the computer next to me. *He looks like someone who knows what he's doing,* I thought. "Hi," I said. "Can you please help me with this?" He looked up from his keyboard. "Sure," he replied. "What do you need help with?" My assumption was correct. His name was Darren.

He just so happened to be a tech prodigy with a background in finance. He leaned across, tapped a few keys, and unlocked the puzzle. Easy! And so, on that calculated note, our relationship began. Statistically speaking, we were on the same page. Socially and economically, we were worlds apart.

Darren's family was rich, sophisticated, and tight-knit. They got on with each other; mine grew further apart by the day. He was a successful startup entrepreneur; I was an undergrad whose dream of making it big in another country had just been shattered. Darren had recently purchased his own spacious apartment. I still lived in my humble childhood home.

He leaned across, tapped a few keys, and unlocked the puzzle. Easy! And so, on that calculated note, our relationship began.

What brought us together was a random act of calculus. What made us stay together, in typical South African fashion, was yet another random act of violence.

We were sitting outside my house in Darren's car one Sunday night. He had come to fetch me after a family fight—a regular occurrence in our household—had turned very physical. I had been locked outside, forced to sit on the sidewalk in our notoriously dangerous neighborhood, on the street where I had been shot only six years earlier. I was telling Darren about the latest altercation with my mother and brother, when I heard a tapping at my window.

I turned to see a gun, pressed against the glass. The tapping grew louder, more urgent. Darren started the engine, shifted into gear, and sped away. His quick thinking very likely saved our lives.

It didn't take long for the crushing reality to set in. Twice in my young life, I'd had a gun pointed at me, steps away from my home. Except, it wasn't my home anymore. I couldn't go back, even if I wanted to. Back to my mother's fury, back to the cruel words, back to the sudden, but now strangely expected, violence. After my father, the rock in my life, had died all those years ago, my mother had told me that I needed to be Moses, leading my family to the Promised Land. Now, the only person I needed to set free, was myself.

Darren invited me to stay in his new apartment. He had just bought the place, and it wasn't furnished yet. But he opened the door to me, and I slept on the wooden floor, with just a pillow and a blanket, for the first week. Every morning, Darren brought me passion fruit juice and a croissant for breakfast. No one had been so kind to me before. I was grateful and overwhelmed. Overnight, I went from knowing one life to beginning another.

My plan was to get back on my feet and move out. I didn't want to be a burden to anyone. But all that changed when Darren asked me to move in with him. I accepted, to his family's dismay. Considering we were all Jewish, you'd think I would fit in, right? Wrong. To them, I came from the wrong side of the tracks.

No matter how many academic, musical, and entrepreneurial accomplishments I had, I wasn't accepted. But Darren wouldn't let his family's opinions get in the way of our relationship.

On the outside, I was strong. But the years of pain and trauma were taking their toll. I couldn't face the world. I felt I had failed. Looking after my family had meant everything to me—by my mother's definition, I was Moses, leading the Jews to the Promised Land

— and now I had cut them out of my life. I wanted to build a new family with Darren, but his family's rejection was too much to bear. If I was Moses, then I had just been sent back to exile in Egypt.

I lost myself in study. It was the one constant in my life, my one hope of redemption. Darren, in his kindness and understanding, knew I needed time to be alone. I would spend day after day in the parking lot, sitting inside Darren's brand-new Mercedes. I stacked binders on the back seat, preparing for my actuarial board exam. I would get in the car at 8 am and would stagger out at sunset.

One day, Darren told me I needed to face the world again. He looked me in the eye and handed me a gift. I opened the box. Inside was a pretty pink iPod. The same color as those roller skates that had caught my eye as a child. I had wanted them so badly. I had worked for them so hard. And when I finally held them in my hands, I had stashed them at the back of a cupboard, unworn and never used. They were a symbol of my longing, and it was enough just to have and to hold them.

Darren had heard me tell the story many times. He knew what that pretty pink color meant to me. But he knew, too, that the real value of a gift is the thoughts it brings to mind. He said he had compiled a special playlist, just for me. I popped in the earbuds and listened, expecting music. Instead, I heard words of wisdom and courage from some of Darren's favorite motivational speakers. He had given me the gift of his inspiration.

I would get in the car at 8am and would stagger out at sunset. One day, Darren told me I needed to face the world again. He looked me in the eye and handed me a gift. I opened the box. Inside was a pretty pink iPod.

It was the breakthrough I needed. I realized I wasn't alone in my feelings of helplessness and despair. And in the words I heard, I found the strength I never knew I had—the strength to carry on. I hadn't given up after my father's death, my mother's abuse, the carjacking, the bullet in my side. Why should I quit now? Not while I had something to offer the world. The gift of my own inspiration.

I had a sought-after degree, and a love of learning instilled in me by my father and grandfather, and the long list of teachers who wanted to bring out the best in me.

In Canada, there was Professor Syd, who looked like Einstein and who loved math as much as I did. I would stay after class, and he would painstakingly lead me through the maze of problems and equations on the board. I felt like an explorer in another universe. At home, I *dreamed* in math. I couldn't wait to get to school in the morning, to pick up where we had left off.

Math was my superpower. What if I could use it to help other people? The paradox of knowledge is that the more you share it, the more it multiplies.

And that was why I became a teacher.

South Africa has one of the worst standards of math and science education in the world. In 2014, the country ranked right at the bottom of the table—144th out of 144 countries—for the quality of its Math and Science education in the World Economic Forum (WEF) Global Competitiveness Report. Partly, this is a legacy of the apartheid system, which segregated schools and applied an inferior education system in black areas.

HF Verwoerd, a Prime Minister known as the "Architect of Apartheid," went as low as stating that black Africans should be "hewers of wood and drawers of water," with their education limited to basic literacy and numeracy.

> *At home, I dreamed in math. I couldn't wait to get back to school in the morning, to pick up where we had left off. Math was my superpower. What if I could use it to help other people?*

As a white South African, I had enjoyed the privilege of the best education at private schools. In my short stay in Canada, I had learned even more. Now I wanted to pay it forward. I had no formal teaching qualification, but the shortage of math and science teachers in South Africa was so dire that I would likely be able to qualify on my degree alone. I dropped off my resume at a few schools in the neighborhood.

The next day, I got a call from a principal. His school was struggling. To make matters worse, the head of the math department (it's called "maths" in South Africa) had been booked off after a cancer diagnosis. I was offered his job. "Can you start tomorrow?" the principal asked. I accepted without hesitation. I was 19, just a couple of years out of school myself. I was tasked with teaching Grade 11 and 12 math.

The Grade 12s had their final exams in eight weeks. Their class average was 27%. Even according to the lenient standards of the education system, where a 30% mark was considered a pass, that was a fail. The principal seemed to have given up all hope of a better result. "Just show up and do your best," he told me. "None of them are going to university anyway."

I walked in the next day to see about 500 students in navy blue and white striped blazers, paired with gray pants. The boys were lined up at the beginning of the school day, waiting to hear the daily announcements. I flashed them a smile. The students stared back, probably confused by who I was and why I was there. My class for the day filed into their classroom.

The principal stood at the front and introduced me as the stand-in head of the math department. There was a short silence as he left the classroom. The boys erupted with energy as I took my place at the board. They wouldn't quiet down.

> *The principal seemed to have given up all hope of a better result. "Just show up and do your best," he told me. "None of them are going to university anyway."*

I was 5'6, a hundred pounds, with an Audrey Hepburn haircut. By their calculation, I was not to be taken seriously. Unfortunately, their math was wrong. I climbed onto a chair and screamed, "Shut up!" They sat down and shut up. Whether I had gotten their attention with respect or surprise, it didn't matter. I was going to hold on to it.

I explained that I wasn't a math teacher. I was a mathematician. I loved mathematics the way other people loved soccer. I told the boys I wanted to give them the same gift. For the next semester, we would do our best. I would treat them as my equals and hopefully, some of them would gain the same appreciation I had for math. They weren't enthusiastic, but they seemed willing to try. I could work with that.

I instructed the boys to move their desks from the usual class layout, into concentric circles. As I presented mathematical concepts, I included real-life, practical applications. I loved writing problems on the board and asking my students to solve them. They could tell my enthusiasm was genuine. Although they weren't filled with the same excitement, I believe they appreciated that I cared.

Preparing my students for their exams wasn't easy. School finished at 2.15 pm every day. I would sit with them until 8, 9, or even 10 pm, working through problems. We would dine on sandwiches, the students and I taking turns to supply the cheap brown bread and the peanut butter and jelly. The groundskeeper would let us into the class on weekends to go over more challenging subjects.

One of the students, Ayanda, had been selected to play football in the U.S. on a sports scholarship. He made it through the trials, but would be turned down if he couldn't pass Grade 12 math. The day I started teaching, his average was 33%. To get his scholarship, he would need at least 50%. We had a long way to go, and very little time. I needed to do whatever it would take to get him there.

Each student in my class had his own story of living through the horrors of apartheid. Many had grown up in the "servants' quarters" of wealthy peoples' homes, where their parents were employed as domestic workers. They were often so underpaid and exploited, that they had to ask their employers to pay for the boys' school uniforms.

My students could easily have adopted the same apathetic attitude our society had taken towards them. Instead, they chose to learn and grow together. Many of them walked me home at night because they cared about my safety. We cared, together, about their future.

In the end, almost every student passed his math exam. Many went on to attend university, an impossible dream just a few months earlier. Ayanda got his scholarship to play sports in the U.S. I stayed in contact with the boys, rejoicing at the new lives they had built for themselves.

I went on to teach at other high schools. At one point, I was teaching at three schools at the same time. To make the schedule work, I hired a driver to drive me from school to school. I got onto the board of the Mathematics Association, as more opportunities came my way.

One day, I was contacted by the School of Banking and Insurance, the feeder University for the banking and insurance industry in South Africa. They asked me to teach their First Year Statistics, Second Year Financial Math, and Third Year Finance students. At the age of 20, I was appointed a full-time guest professor at a university.

In the little free time I had, I continued studying for my board exams. My goal hadn't changed. I would teach until I passed the tests, and I would take up a well-paying job in banking. But what job, exactly? I was asked to take a career suitability test at a financial training organization. No problem, I thought. I love tests! Especially ones you can't fail.

> *Many of them walked me home at night*
> *because they cared about my safety.*
> *We cared, together, about their future.*

I had never failed an exam in my life, but I considered this career suitability test a failure. I had been trained as an actuary. My results said I was a researcher and entrepreneur. This freaked me out, as much as spooked the training organization. They came back with crushing news. I was unemployable.

"We can't hire you," I was told. "We don't want you empowering these bankers through licensing exams." It sounds crazy, but it's an honest concern. Why would they want someone to come in and motivate their bankers to find outside financial solutions? I had to reexamine my life. I had been happy about who I was and what I was doing, for two main reasons. Teaching, and Darren.

Standing in front of a class, with chalk in my hand, gave me a high. It was the same feeling I had when performing in an orchestra as a kid. But instead of playing the cello, which I hated, I was speaking passionately about topics I cared about. I walked the path of discovery alongside my students, guiding them on their educational journey. Every day I was helping people, and they, in turn, were helping me.

As for Darren, he helped me in more ways than I could imagine. Beyond the material items and emotional support, he helped me find my strength. It wasn't long before we were able to combine our knowledge and strength to build things together.

I spent years mulling over the results of my career assessment test. I had been designated as unemployable, but those keywords rang in my ears. "Researcher" and "Entrepreneur." The most important word in that sequence being: *and*. I wondered what it would mean to combine the two. One day, it came to me in the form of an equation:

Researcher + Entrepreneur = Investor

I had found the formula that would change my life. And I knew if I used it in the right way, that I could help to change the lives of others.

Learn the Skills You Never Knew You Had

"Pizza party!" At the end of every semester, the call went out. We would cast aside our textbooks and forget about math and statistics for a while, as we feasted on triangles sliced out of a circle. You see, I would tell my students, math is everywhere! But as much as I loved sharing my insights, and seeing the sparkle in a student's eye when they made the connection between ancient theory and the real world, I knew my destiny did not lie in the formal confines of academia.

I longed to make an impact in the real world myself, and that breakthrough equation kept on playing in my mind. *Researcher + Entrepreneur = Investor.* Teaching gave me a platform to voice my opinions and insights. It allowed me to foster the hope of a better life for my bright-eyed students, in a society where more than half of young people were out of work.

> *I knew my destiny did not lie in the formal confines of academia. I longed to make an impact in the real world myself, and that breakthrough equation kept on playing in my mind. Researcher + Entrepreneur = Investor.*

I would regularly bump into my former students, doing their best to eke out a living as cashiers or sales consultants in retail stores. Sometimes I would see a graduate, in cap and gown, standing at a traffic light, holding up a cardboard sign displaying their qualifications, along with a plea for a job. Any job. It broke my heart. Education alone wasn't enough to put them on the road to sustenance and success. Even with their university degrees, they would have to build their own businesses if they wanted financial independence.

The key to unlocking that better life, I came to realize, was leverage. In business, leverage typically refers to one of two things. It's either the power you hold in a situation, or the beneficial ratio of outputs and inputs in your work. To be successful in your field, you need both.

Once you've achieved a leveraged position, you can scale your business, or increase its size and scope. These principles can lead to wealth creation. I knew what they were, but I needed to find an effective way to apply them.

Entrepreneurship had given me a ticket out of economic struggle, out of a negative mindset, and for a while, out of my home country. Now I was back, and I was looking for a bigger ticket. A golden ticket, to echo the quest in Roald Dahl's story of Willy Wonka. And I found it, once again, close to home, in Johannesburg, my city of gold.

One day, Darren told me he had inherited a commercial building from his late uncle. It had opened the door to a long-standing ambition: to buy property at the lowest possible price, fix it up, and resell at a handsome profit. Wholesale real estate investment, it's called, or more commonly, flipping. I was intrigued. I wanted to be a flipper too.

I told Darren about my childhood obsession with the Midrand Corridor, the vast tract of undeveloped land between Johannesburg, where I lived, and Pretoria, where my dad had his shop. If only the bank hadn't turned down my request for a loan. True, I was just a kid. But a kid with a dream. And now I had a chance to make it come true.

Darren had degrees in Finance and Law. I had a degree in Statistics and Actuarial Science. We teamed up and bought out our first property, a repossessed building, at a Sheriff's auction. It was a bargain, run-down and in desperate need of work, but with huge potential resale value.

I remember my hand shaking as I took out the checkbook. Partly from nerves—we hadn't even been allowed to inspect the property before the auction—but also from excitement. We were in business. Real business. The brick-and-mortar kind.

> *I was looking for a bigger ticket. A golden ticket, to echo the quest in Roald Dahl's story of Willy Wonka. And I found it, once again, very close to home, in Johannesburg, my city of gold.*

Darren and I would analyze likely neighborhoods, collecting data and making projections. We would make site visits, stopping by local grocery stores to get a feel for the area. I used a tool we had developed ourselves, similar to Zillow, to help with research. Our science was rough, but the potential return on investment was high. If we could make it work, we could create something scalable that would also help lift these areas out of poverty.

It was hard to see much promise or potential in the places we bought. Most units didn't have electricity or hot water. Every inch was coated in dirt or debris. It was going to take a lot of work to make the properties presentable.

Luckily, Darren had excellent taste and a flair for design. I spent hours training my eyes to visualize what our marketing material would define as "gorgeous and aspirational." We prepared to recreate these "fixer-upper" spaces using Darren's five-star vision and my obsession with keeping costs to a minimum. That meant doing everything ourselves.

We secured building and interior supplies at cost or slightly above. No easy feat, given how primitive the internet was back then. We aimed for the quickest turnaround. Two to four weeks for small properties, and six to 12 weeks for large. To further cut costs, Darren and I took on the construction work. I often came home exhausted, covered in soil, paint, and dust, my back and head aching. For jobs requiring specialized skills, we brought in workers.

Every one of us worked seven days a week, from 7 am to 10 pm. Darren and I learned a lot about leadership, and worked hard to earn the respect of our small team. As we learned the hard way, there's a process to building or rebuilding a house.

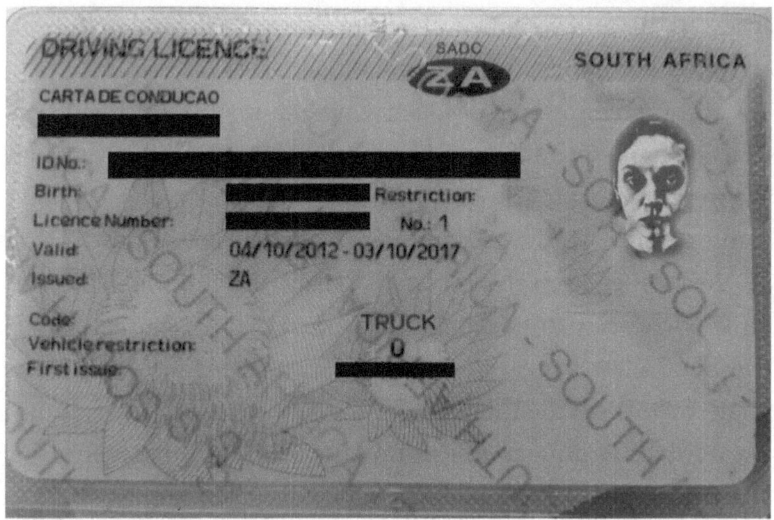

When we were flipping residential properties in Johannesburg, getting supplies delivered on time was a constant frustration. I realized we need a dedicated trucker on our team. But who? Sometimes, the best way to get things done is to do the trucking job yourself.

You can't put up a roof until the trusses are installed, but you can't install the trusses until the walls are framed. You can't reframe the walls until you've installed the plumbing and the wiring. Each task depends on another task. If even one supplier is delayed, nothing gets done. We couldn't sit around, waiting for other people to do the jobs that had to be done before all the other jobs could be done.

When we battled to get supplies in time, I realized we needed a dedicated trucker on our team. I had never driven a truck in my life. That was reason enough to learn. I passed the test for my trucker's license and picked up the supplies myself. Trucking across town was fun and empowering. I felt like I could do anything.

I applied logistical techniques to our deliveries, cutting costs and saving time. On a traditional build, we might wait up to four days for bricks and other essential materials to be delivered. Most people accepted this and kept their people onsite, waiting for deliveries to arrive. In our minds, this was silly.

We wanted to run a productive operation, just like the American companies we admired. Every day of lost time cost us money. We weren't going to let our properties stand idle. With each build completed, we faced a new and even bigger challenge. Sales.

In another effort to cut costs, we marketed and sold our properties ourselves, cutting out the 7% fee paid to real estate agents. We consulted a few, but each told us our target asking price was crazy. They couldn't see the value we saw in these properties. Thankfully, Darren is a consummate salesman. And I had learned the ropes too, all the way back when I sold my dad's old suits to raise the cash to buy my pretty pink roller skates.

Without a real estate agent to guide and advise us, we had to figure out how to stage each property for viewing. We raided our own home furniture, which meant living months at a time with just a bed in our apartment — and that was only because the bed was too big and heavy to carry.

By day, Darren would be working on his solo business venture. In the evening, he would design the kitchens, bathrooms, and bedrooms from scratch. His daytime business was a successful digital design company, which gave him the keen eye we needed. He was the chief architect.

There was no IKEA in South Africa. Any furniture or built-in cabinetry we needed, had to be made by hand. We would stay up late, cutting, drilling, and assembling. After the hardcore building work was done, I would decorate a property, which required a great deal of creativity.

How do you recreate those homes in Wallpaper and Architectural Digest, on a dime? I used an unusual skill I had acquired while working in the costume shop. I would buy fake ostrich skin fabric and secure it with packing tape onto the hall tables. It lent an exotic and aspirational look that worked.

Once the cabinets were installed, each piece of furniture was laid out, and the gardens were landscaped, it was time for show days. Darren would host buyers on the Sunday afternoon following the completion of the home. We would entice viewers with drinks, snacks, and cool jazz ballads by Frank Sinatra. We wanted to make them feel right at home. And we wanted to make a name for ourselves too.

SP Properties had been born, its name adopted from Darren's digital agency. The first show day filled me with anxiety. I sat outside in my car, waiting to hear the reactions of potential buyers. Did they like what we created? Did they want to buy? More importantly, would they be prepared to pay our asking price? To our great relief and delight, the answer to all three questions, more often than not, was a big, resounding *yes*.

People would walk into the properties and fall in love. Many were willing to pay a healthy premium just to be able to move in. Some asked if they could move in, as is. They wanted to keep the staged pictures on the walls, the curtains, cushions, and furniture, just as we had it.

One prospective buyer lay down on our glamorous "Beverly Hills Mansion Style" bed, only to fall straight to the floor. It was an airbed, propped up on empty boxes—the very definition of marketing a dream out of thin air.

Most people closed their deal without any issue. Even so, we found new meaning in the old phrase, "it's not over until the money is in the bank." We were renting one of our units to a tenant, who came to us one day with an offer to buy. He seemed a little too eager, but given that he was offering a substantial premium in cash, we said yes and signed the contract.

> *One prospective buyer lay down on our glamorous "Beverly Hills Mansion Style" bed, only to fall straight to the floor. It was an airbed, propped up on empty boxes.*

After everything was finalized, he appeared to pull out of the deal. Using our newly acquired legal skills, we wrote him a letter threatening to sue. The money arrived in our bank account 24 hours later and the deal was done. Years later, we found out he was wanted by Interpol for human trafficking. A lesson learned — always trust your gut!

As our sales and portfolio grew, SP Properties became a force in the South African real estate market. Other companies were impressed by our quick turnaround time and low building costs.

We invested in pricier homes that attracted upscale clients, among them the executives of McKinsey and Porsche, and a couple of well-heeled investors from the U.S. To celebrate, Darren bought me a Cartier diamond necklace, with a beautiful heart-shaped pendant. I've worn it ever since. We'd both put our hearts into the business, and our sweat and toil too.

We managed to make it through the 2008-2009 financial crisis, but our costs kept soaring as the South African currency plummeted, amidst rising political instability. We knew the smart thing to do was sell our business.

I'd had my first experience of hands-on, high-stakes entrepreneurship. I'd learned how to run a successful, scalable company. I'd learned to paint, build, drive a truck, and decorate a property. I knew that volatility was the only certainty in business, and that the only way to ride the waves of change was to diversify. Now came the next big challenge. I was going to have to learn to survive and thrive in an invisible world.

The world of digital entrepreneurship.

SEVEN

Make a Dent in the Universe

The man in the gown stands at the podium, glancing down at his notes on a sunny California day. With his salt-and-pepper beard, receding hairline, and rimless glasses, he looks suitably professorial as he addresses the gathering of grads. But the truth is, he's a college dropout, and beneath the academic gown, he is wearing jeans and open-toed sandals. Nobody seems to mind.

The young students, about to embark on the next stage of their great journey through life, look up in adoration, hanging onto his every word. He is talking about the power of love.

"You've got to find what you love," he says. "And that is as true for your work as it is for your lovers. The only way to do great work is to love what you do. If you haven't found it yet, keep looking. Don't settle. As with all matters of the heart, you'll know when you find it."

The man in the gown, the college dropout, is Steve Jobs, co-founder of Apple and one of the most successful and influential entrepreneurs in history. The year is 2005, and he is delivering the commencement address at Stanford University. Over and over I would watch him, mesmerized, hitting pause on YouTube, taking notes, until I could recite every word of his address by heart. *Find what you love. Keep looking. Don't settle.*

> *Over and over I would watch him, mesmerized, hitting pause on YouTube, taking notes, until I could recite every word of his address by heart. Find what you love. Keep looking. Don't settle.*

I was a long, long way from Silicon Valley, but I could feel the seismic waves of the tech revolution, which had arrived in my home country of South Africa in the same year as our transition to democracy. In 1994, when apartheid was abolished and Nelson Mandela was inaugurated as President, the sweep of freedom brought with it two mighty forces of unfettered communication. Mobile telephony, and the internet. Those who could see the future were already riding the wave. And Darren was right there among them.

By 2010, the year of the FIFA World Cup in South Africa—another sign of our re-entry into the global arena—Darren was the co-owner of one of the country's top digital agencies. He and his team had built and implemented over 600 large-scale enterprise projects for some of the biggest companies in the world, including Anheuser-Busch, Coke, Pepsi, Sony, and Porsche. I was fascinated by Darren's work. He'd tell me about his important clients and the future of the "digital age."

When he asked if I'd be interested in starting a digital marketing company with him, I was overjoyed. "Yes!" I shouted. With Darren's background in the field and my obsession with data and analytics, we made a winning team once again.

Staging and selling homes had given me experience in the fixed realm of real estate, but I needed to acquaint myself with the limitless universe of the virtual. I took a Google certification course on marketing, and it made all the difference in the world. Just like that, we started our new company, Digital By Design. I was the co-founder and "Head of Strategy and Innovation." It was official. I was an innovator.

I read every white paper I could get my hands on. I became a huge fan of companies like HubSpot. We were restlessly opportunistic, always on the lookout for a scalable version of what Darren was building for his Fortune 500 clients. In this brave new world, data was gold.

While other South African technology companies were building websites, we were on a quest to find a unique clientele who understood our mission. We knew that data was our primary asset. I used my analytical skill to optimize our clients' campaigns and branding, engaging with consumers in new and exciting ways.

Unlike other advertising, PR, and communications agencies, who were still using focus groups and run-of-the-mill campaigns, we were taking a page out of Google's handbook. *Use data!*

I wanted Digital By Design to emulate Google in every way. Just like them, we wanted PhDs working on our team. Trying to find PhDs in South Africa with the skills we needed, an interest in what we were doing, and at a cost we could afford, was almost impossible. I posted on South Africa's version of Craigslist: "Physics PhD graduates Wanted for Exciting, World-Class Marketing Roles." Only the brave—or the crazy—applied.

Hiring in South Africa meant competing against Fortune 500 companies, who could pay big bucks that we couldn't. Still, our business was growing. We had 70 employees and two divisions: Enterprise Solutions, and Social Media & S.E.O, or Search Engine Optimization.

Darren ran Enterprise Solutions, the hardcore side of the business. As a world-class salesman, he was able to convince big multinational pharma clients to let us run their online marketing. At the same time, we were burning through money. We desperately needed to slash our overhead costs. And, just as desperately, we needed to grow.

In yet another crazy attempt to be like Google, we set up a six-month internship program. We gave our interns live clients, whose sites needed optimizing. We measured their performance. If the interns were effective, they were hired as full-time employees. If not, they would have gained sought-after experience in a growing field. As cut-throat as it seems, the program was a massive success. We had a waiting list to join. Other companies came to us, asking if we'd build them a similar internship program. If only we had the time.

I posted adverts on South Africa's version of Craigslist: "Physics PhD graduates Wanted for Exciting, World-Class Marketing Roles." Only the brave or crazy applied.

The hours were brutal. When I wasn't working with interns or clients, I was in my office, researching, calculating, mining data. Our offices were originally at Regus on Sandton Square, a high-end address in South Africa's wealthiest square mile of real estate. We shared offices with such multinationals as Bain, McKinsey, and Louis Vuitton. Until, one day, we were asked to leave. It was my fault: I was watching too much YouTube. I was consuming more bandwidth than all those other companies combined.

The management at Regus didn't believe I was watching those videos for work purposes. I tried to explain that we were building a digital marketing agency, focusing on data and analytics. In their minds, I was watching cat videos at their expense. But Darren and I had a better place in mind.

It was a property we'd kept for ourselves, after selling SP Properties. We had invested a lot of money in the space, installing ponds, waterfalls, Zen gardens, and a magnificent open-floor office, overlooking a river. It became the new headquarters of Digital by Design.

It was an exciting experiment. It sounds corny to say "our company is a family," but in our case, it was true. Working in a house changes the office dynamic. Our employees were skilled and enthusiastic. We wanted to make sure everyone felt respected and fulfilled on our journey towards a common goal.

Just like Google, we provided our staff with a plethora of amenities, including a swimming pool, a sunlit outdoor space, and bean bag chairs in front of the communal TV. There was a cottage in the back for staff to sleep over when working late. If they preferred, they could sit outside in the sunshine and work. They got to choose the office playlist.

Our partnership with the beer brand, Anheuser-Busch, gave our staff access to live, high-profile music events by global superstars. One of the most memorable performances was a Drake concert. We helped create the campaigns.

Our beverage clients were generous, delivering weekly orders of whatever we requested. Our staff took home crates of free drinks every week. These amenities fostered creativity and happiness in the workplace. Turns out, if you invest in your employees, creating a positive atmosphere in pursuit of a common goal, you can find great success in business. Our big-name clients were thrilled with the results. The list kept growing.

Roche, Bayer Healthcare, Pepsi, Anheuser-Busch, Coca-Cola, Citibank, Bank of America, Prudential Financial, Deloitte, Ernst & Young, Rolls-Royce, Aston Martin, Porsche, BMW, Nissan.

Companies we admired wanted to partner with us. We won more clients from overseas. That same year, I was voted one of the three most Inspiring Women in Tech in the UK. I began researching opportunities in the UK and Europe, but I had my heart set on the U.S. I was obsessed with Google and Silicon Valley.

"You can't connect the dots looking forward," the man at the podium had said. "You can only connect them looking backward. You have to trust in something—your gut, destiny, life, karma, whatever. This approach has never let me down, and it has made all the difference in my life."

I wanted to be like Steve Jobs. I wanted to be where he had been, to stand where he had stood. I wanted to walk through the valley.

And just like him, whatever it took, I wanted to make a dent in the universe.

I wanted to be where he had been, to stand where he had stood. I wanted to walk through the valley. And just like him, whatever it took, I wanted to make a dent in the universe.

Conquer Your Fear of the Faraway Horizon

It was a bright, cold day in Washington, D.C., and Darren was behind the wheel of our rental car, driving on the wrong side of the road. Well, the right side, which took some getting used to because in South Africa we drive on the left. "This feels weird," said Darren, as he navigated the bustle of traffic on the way to our meeting. I was sitting in the passenger seat, taking deep breaths in a bid to calm my nerves.

There was a lot at stake, and I still wasn't convinced we were making the right move. But it was too late to back out now.

Be careful what you wish for, I thought. And then, with a jolt, I caught sight of flashing blue and red lights in the wing mirror. The ear-splitting whoop of a siren, and the raging voice of law and order: "Pull over! Pull over right now!" Darren pulled over. I was nervous. I had seen enough American movies and TV shows to know that being pulled over by a cop in a patrol car hardly ever ends well. What had we done?

The cop strode over to the driver's side, and motioned Darren to roll down the window. "Good morning, Sir," he said. Everyone in America was so polite. But there was a steely edge to this politeness. "Do you know what you just did?" Darren shrugged. "Sorry, Officer," he said. "I'm not really sure." The cop narrowed his gaze. "You almost ran over a pedestrian. License and registration." I was shocked. What pedestrian? I pictured us being thrown out of the country, bringing our dream of a new start – our first global entrepreneurial venture – to a crashing halt. The cop studied Darren's papers.

"You're from Africa?" Darren nodded and forced a friendly smile. "South Africa," he said. The cop thought hard. He looked at me. "Morning, Ma'am," he said. So polite. He leaned on the window frame. "Do they teach you how to drive over pedestrians, back in Africa?" Suddenly, I remembered.

We had swerved around a guy on the crosswalk, without thinking too much about it. Now, we were thinking. Darren could talk his way out of anything. I had seen it many times. But could he talk his way out of a charge of reckless driving, as a citizen of a foreign country?

The cop strode over to the driver's side, and motioned Darren to roll down the window. "Good morning, Sir," he said. Everyone in America was so polite. But there was a steely edge to this politeness. "Do you know what you just did?"

"Well, you see, Officer," he explained, "In South Africa you can drive around pedestrians. As long as you never hit them." The cop looked horrified. But he believed us. "Just remember," he said, "You're in America now. And over here, you need to respect pedestrians and obey the rules of the road. Have a good day now!"

And so we drove, keeping a watchful eye out for pedestrians, to meet the Venture Capital firm we hoped would invest in our new tech startup, which was already a big success back home. It had started as a spin-off of Digital By Design. We had been approached by three Fortune 500 companies: the world's leading ophthalmic lens provider, the world's largest beer company, and a global pharma company. They all had a unique sales problem that required our help.

On the outside, their quandaries seemed radically different. But the solution we came up with was the same. A sales enablement app, allowing companies to track and analyze customer engagement, while connecting customers to sales reps with ease. We called it Acceleforce, as in, "Accelerate YOUR Sales Force!" As with so many big ideas, it was as simple as it was revolutionary.

We built it as a SaaS (Software as a Service) platform. If Acceleforce could increase sales by just 10%, it would be worth the investment. A

10% increase in sales for all three companies would amount to well over a billion dollars. If we could achieve that goal for them, what would their investment be? Fifty million? A hundred million? More?

We wrote up the patent applications, figuring out the logistics as we went along. Acceleforce had a natural momentum, different from anything we'd done before. When we told other clients about it, they all wanted access.

Companies ranging from healthcare, insurance, and financial services were willing to pay significant sums to be early customers. Within the first year, we earned over $400,000 in revenue. Darren and I wanted to bring on extra team members, but it was hard to source the skills we needed. We leveraged Kaggle competitions to recruit talent from the U.S., Greece, Russia, UAE, and Israel.

Acceleforce stoked a fire that had been raging in me for years. I wanted to make it big in the United States. Each opportunity that arose, I would ask myself, is this it? Can this be the one? I believed Acceleforce was our ticket out. I knew it was a risk worth taking.

There was a glimmer of a possibility that our innovation could secure us a spot in Silicon Valley, the dream capital of my American obsession. "You're crazy!" people told me. No one believed that two South Africans like us would be able to succeed in the U.S. In South Africa, we were big fish in a small pond. We were savvy business people with a successful, comfortable life. Why would we move to a big, scary place like America, just to pitch a sales app?

My father used to tell me the story of his journey by boat from a little village in Lithuania. He set foot with the rest of his family in a strange and distant land on the edge of the African continent. I used to think to myself, why did they get on the wrong boat? If they had fled to the USA, I would have been born an American. But it wasn't too late for a do over.

"You're crazy!" people told me. No one believed that two South Africans like us would be able to succeed in the U.S. In South Africa, we were big fish in a small pond.

The transition wasn't easy. Though I knew the story of America was a story of immigrants who had come from all over the world, we felt like another species altogether. We felt like strangers. Even in the most everyday situations, we battled to find a way to fit in.

When Darren lost his wallet in the subway one day, we stood in line at the Lost & Found at Union Station. I was wearing a pair of fancy shoes I'd bought for the 50th wedding anniversary of Darren's parents. As we chatted in the queue, I could feel someone looking down at me.

"Excuse me," she said, "are you African?" For a moment, I felt excited — we had been recognized! "Yes," I said. "Are you South African?" she asked. Now I was really excited. She had even recognized my accent, far away from home. "Yes!" She asked how long we had been in the U.S. We chatted for a while, and then the conversation took an odd turn. "So what's it like to wear shoes?" she asked. Excuse me? "You're African, what's it like to wear shoes on your feet for the first time?"

I was stunned into silence, but Darren wasn't going to leave it there. "These are my first shoes too!" he said, pointing at his feet. "Isn't it incredible? We don't even have blisters!" We laughed about it afterwards, but at the time, I felt judged by a total stranger who hadn't walked a mile in my shoes. Was this what America was going to be like?

Then, one day, I saw news of a competition: the Guardian Activate NYC Summit. They were looking for "game-changing startups in 1 of 5 industries to be chosen as a finalist." If chosen, you would pitch your startup to the CEOs and CTOs of some of the biggest tech companies in the world. I let the application sit there for days. I was too intimidated to apply.

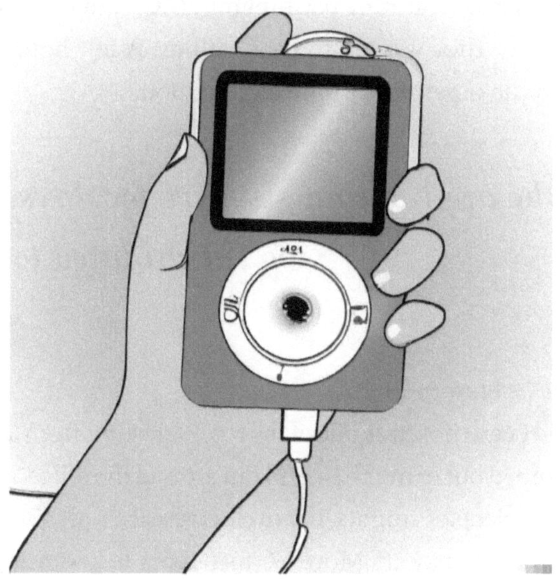

On that pink iPod Darren had given me, all those years ago, I had heard a talk by Tony Robbins. I had learned to make a list of daily tasks, and to follow them through. Always. Now, for the first time, I was stuck with two tasks I was unable to complete:

1.   Apply for VC funding
2.   Submit entry for Guardian Activate NYC Summit

Day after day, it was killing me. My fear was holding me back. I heard Tony's voice in my head. "Step up! Step Up! Step Up!" At 9 am on a Monday morning, I sat down and made a list of the top venture capitalists and accelerator programs in the U.S. There were 40 names. I emailed each a pitch of our startup. Darren sat beside me to help answer the questions for the Guardian Activate NYC Summit. The next day, we got a reply. A General Partner of a VC-funded accelerator in Washington, D.C. said they liked what we were up to. They wanted to chat with us. A few hours later, we heard from the organizers of the competition.

I let the application sit there for days. I was too intimidated to apply.

The news blew me away.

We had been chosen as one of the top 10 startups from around the globe. I jumped out of my chair and ran around the office, screaming with joy. The sleepless nights, my tireless research, all our sacrifices, were beginning to pay off. More VC firms emailed, wanting to learn more about Acceleforce. We had choices! But first, we had to turn our energies to the competition. We had to be in New York in a week.

As Darren and I drove away from JFK, I felt a familiar anxiety. I was reminded of my car ride to the English toy factory. Then I was just a child, afraid of the foreign countryside. Now I was an adult, cowering at the sight of the Microsoft building. The self-doubt started kicking in. I was terrified I would destroy both our lives. I squeezed Darren's hand. He squeezed mine back.

On the day before the competition, we sat in our hotel room, practicing the pitch. We had done countless sales pitches, but an "investor pitch" was a whole new thing. When we walked in the next day, the hall was packed. Crowds didn't scare us, but what happened next was a nightmare. Darren stood at the podium and spoke into the mic. There was no sound. It was like watching a train crash in slow motion. I was sitting in the safety of the audience. I wanted the ground to open beneath my feet. Darren regained his composure and spoke loudly enough for some of the audience to hear, but it was too late. He was off his game. The presentation was a washout. We left the competition disappointed, but not without hope.

We returned to our hotel room to finish the final round of interviews with VCs. We zeroed in on three choices. There was the Tony Hsieh accelerator program in Las Vegas, a VC fund in Silicon Valley, and the first VC who had contacted us from D.C. We chose the D.C. VC and hopped on a train.

After our encounter with the cop and the pedestrian, we stopped by our VC's offices. We were horrified by what we found. A cold, dark attic at the top of a bank building. Empty cleaning bottles were strewn about. The place looked like a crime scene. The VCs began dodging our calls, canceling every meeting we set up. We were on our own. The partners had seemed like nice guys. We felt comfortable with them, and we believed the fit would work. We wanted it to work. But we made the wrong choice.

Coming from South Africa, we never had a clue. We failed to do the proper due diligence. It was an expensive mistake, never to be repeated. When we signed on, they promised us the world. Now they were nowhere to be seen. Going back home to South Africa was no longer an option. It would mean admitting defeat. "Hustle, hustle, hustle! Network, network, network!" I chanted the mantra to myself. We were on a 24/7 work-cycle, burning through cash.

We stopped by our VC's offices. We were horrified by what we found. A cold, dark attic at the top of a bank building. Empty cleaning bottles were strewn about. The place looked like a crime scene.

My insomnia would wake me at 2 am, after only four hours of sleep. I would do yoga, shower, and start my day. Our neighbor would hear the water running and would bang on the ceiling. The walls were paper thin. We were terrified we were going to fail and go home with our tails between our legs. We called my mother-in-law for a little moral support. Instead, we got a lecture.

"You need to stop with this nonsense building companies in America," she said. "Who do you think you are, Bill Gates? Put your feet on the ground, stop this nonsense, and just start behaving like grown-ups now!"

Of course, she said it with love, in the manner of all good Jewish mothers-in-law. We took her words as inspiration. No, we weren't Bill Gates. But we weren't going to give up that easily, either.

We were working harder than ever, leveraging every opportunity we could. *Hustle, hustle, hustle!* I went into deep research mode. I completed an executive education program at Harvard, granting me admission into the Harvard Club of Washington, D.C. Through my connections, I was appointed chair of AlmaLinks, a global organization of CEOs. *Network, network, network!*

Darren and I found a reprieve at a new accelerator in D.C., called *1776.* The name gave me hope. It stood for liberty, independence, a fresh start. The accelerator's funding came from the founders themselves. They had each built unicorn companies of their own. Their offices were in a shared space of industry leaders, long before the days of WeWork. Only world-class companies were allowed to join. Once you were in, you could talk to anyone. We pitched to T Scott Case, the founding CTO of Priceline.com. We practiced our pitch to President Obama when he came to visit the accelerator.

We worked with top advisors, who were closing deals in the tens of millions. Darren and I interviewed 250 executives, thought leaders, and key decision makers with buying power across all industries. The phone was ringing off the hook. Acceleforce came at the perfect time.

The ability to optimize a sales force was the difference between sink or swim in the new digital era. We were so busy growing, pitching enterprise customer after enterprise customer, building, building, that we ignored the investor calls. We had enough on our plate as it was.

We connected with a fellow entrepreneur, Professor Tom Miller, the Senior Vice Provost for Entrepreneurship at NC State University. He invited us, along with industry partners like Redhat, to base our offices on their new campus. The partnership allowed us to collaborate with the Institute for Advanced Analytics. In return, they gave us their top Data Science graduates. At one point, we were in talks with the NSA (the National Security Agency) about a collaboration. All this attention landed us an offer from the biggest clinical research organization in the world.

With over 40% of the global pharma sales enablement market, they saw the value of Acceleforce and wanted to deploy it in key regions across the globe. They were so excited by what we were doing that they wanted us to move into their offices and acquire exclusivity of our technology. We consulted an attorney. He told us to quote $5 million for a license.

To make all this work, we wound up living in motels in North Carolina. We were waiting for new visas. Without them, we wouldn't be able to carry on working in the USA. And until we had the right documentation, no one in Raleigh would rent us an apartment.

For now, every day, we began our commute to D.C. at 4 am. We drank Love's Travel Stops French Vanilla Cappuccino alongside the truckers, and stopped off at Starbucks for our daily Spinach, Feta & Egg White Wrap. Sometimes we wouldn't get home until 2 am. We'd move from one motel to the next, carrying black garbage bags with our belongings. But we carried something else with us, something we bore on our shoulders like Atlas bearing the weight of the world. We carried the hope that someday, the big deal would break, and that we would be free to stay in America, the land of our dreams.

That day dawned with a multi-million-dollar deal on the line. I had it all planned. We would rise before the sun, at 5.30 am. We would go over the last details of the proposal. We would pack the trash bags with our things, and start loading the van. By 10 am, we would be ready to move. I would go to the front desk with Junior to check out.

Junior, or Junie, was our beloved companion, a sweet-natured brown-and-white bunny rabbit who traveled from place to place with us, all over the USA. In some cultures, rabbits are symbols of prosperity, abundance, and good luck. Just what we needed. But Junie saw things differently.

Darren was on the phone, trying to finalize our pending purchase of a penthouse in Chapel Hill, North Carolina. It was a beautiful space, overlooking a golf course, surrounded by a forest and walking trails, in a sought-after area known as the Research Triangle, home to the highest numbers of PhDs per capita in the world.

Our plan—our dream—was that we would use part of the money from our business deal to move there. As soon as we had closed the deal, we would settle into the penthouse, fly back to South Africa, get our visas approved at the U.S. Embassy, and fly back to our new home. The clock was ticking. And Junie, it turned out, had no interest at all in our plan.

"Junie!" I called, "Come on, Junie!" I was on my knees, staring at the bunny under the bed. I was using my baby voice, my pitch getting higher and higher, and more and more desperate. I tried begging. I tried pleading. I tried coaxing Junie with his favorite treats: carrots, apricots, raisins. I tried sweeping him from under the bed with a broom. I tried lifting the bed. The bunny wouldn't budge. "JUNIE! COME ON, JUNIE!"

The phone rang. It was the front desk, telling us we needed to check out. "Are you coming?" said Darren. "They're going to kick us out!"

I looked up, and had a flash of inspiration. There was a box of motel-branded matches on the floor. I knew that rabbits were mesmerized by a burning flame. No, wait, wasn't that moths? Either way, it was worth a try. I struck a light and held the match under the bed. I switched my voice from baby to hypnotist. "Come to the light, Junie," I whispered. "Come to me, Junie!"

And out he hopped, and off to the meeting we went, smelling like homeless people. The meeting went well. What didn't go well was the trip back to South Africa. It was supposed to be a quick visit. It turned into a bureaucratic disaster. Our visa process was put under administrative review. We were stuck in South Africa for nine weeks. We did our best to keep things running in the U.S., but the lost time made that virtually impossible.

> *I struck a light and held the match under the bed. I switched my voice from baby to hypnotist. "Come to the light, Junie," I whispered.*
>
> *"Come to me, Junie!"*

Darren took daily trips to the U.S. Embassy in Johannesburg. Each time they said, "No news." Nothing to do but wait. Junie, meanwhile, was staying with a "bunnysitter" back in North Carolina. We couldn't wait to see him again. But would we?

We were stuck in limbo on the other side of the world, due to what we discovered was an error we had made on our business visa applications. Friends told us frightening stories of people who hadn't been able to renew their visas. They had to give up on their American dreams. But Darren and I could never do that.

After recruiting an attorney, we applied for a new visa with a 400-page document, proving our value to the U.S. It worked. We were granted a new visa, and we booked the first flight back. Darren and I quickly made up for lost time.

We continued our sleepless night, 24/7 work cycle to put us back on track. It was then that I began to fully comprehend why we had made it. The roadblocks and the naysayers had fueled us. The moments of self-doubt had never slowed us down.

Our only regret was selling Acceleforce too early. One of our big pharma clients wanted to acquire the business as a strategic investment. For us, it made sense. We were playing in the big leagues, with more to come. Moving to the U.S. taught me a lot about myself. I was bright-eyed, optimistic, energized, and unafraid to charge into unfamiliar territory. I had everything it took to be an American.

Watch out, pedestrians — here I come!

NINE

Let Your Voice be Heard Around the World

On our way from the airport to the city center, on a blazing hot summer day, I gazed out of the window and read the writing on the walls. Here and there were the pockmarks of bullet holes, scars of a civil war that had raged for almost three decades. An entire generation had grown up in its shadow. But these reminders of humanity at its worst were outshone by the colors of life at its brightest and most vital.

The walls were painted with portraits of basketball stars, hip hop deejays, Sci-Fi robots, wild animals, SpongeBob SquarePants, Michael Jackson, Nelson Mandela, a woman proudly wearing the map of Africa on her head, and of course, a pair of angel wings that you could stand between for a selfie.

In the universal language of street art and graffiti, I felt right at home, back on the continent where I was born. I was in Luanda, capital of Angola, on a mission to uplift, inform, and inspire. I had come to realize these were my gifts and my calling, and I was willing to travel anywhere in the world to fulfill them. My platform: the Global FiresideChat, a weekly online radio broadcast for entrepreneurs, investors, businesses, educational institutions, governments, NGOs, and corporations.

The name was a tribute to the famous Fireside Chats given on radio by U.S. President Franklin D. Roosevelt, from the years of the Great Depression to the Second World War. "The only thing we have to fear," he told a nation during its darkest hours, "is fear itself."

But the FDR quote that resonated strongest with me was one that seemed to capture the very essence of what it takes to be an entrepreneur. "It isn't sufficient just to want. You've got to ask yourself what you are going to do to get the things you want." The more I thought about it, the more I believed I could get what I wanted by helping and inspiring others to get what they wanted too.

In South Africa, we know this concept as Ubuntu. It means that we are only human through the connections we make with other humans. We reach each other, we teach each other, we learn from each other. In business, we know this simply as networking.

> *The more I thought about it, the more I believed I could get what I wanted by helping and inspiring others to get what they wanted too. In South Africa, we know this concept as Ubuntu.*

My Global FiresideChats were a practical way of putting this concept to the test. I could sit down with one person at a time—a leader in thought and deed, from anywhere in the world—and at the same time, I could talk to millions. Come, sit by the fireside with me, and let's chat. This had all come about as a direct result of the work we were doing with Accelforce, our sales solution platform. I had been invited to become a UN Women Empower Women Global Champion.

We had just sold the company, and I was reassessing my role in business when I received this honor. I wasn't a quiet investor who stayed behind the scenes. I was a cheerleader, an evangelist, rallying anyone who would listen around a common goal. The UN's recognition of my work reaffirmed our belief that my influence should be publicized. I began looking for an outlet to fulfill my new role in Women's empowerment.

I thought of my friend, Jeff Scott Goldman, an Emmy-winning journalist and producer for CBS. He had worked at the White House, covering six presidents. Jeff taught me so much about media. I would take long breaks from my work at Acceleforce to join Jeff on walks. He would share exciting stories about his day. He had extensive knowledge of U.S. history, politics, and economics. He had been an eyewitness to important historical events.

> *I wasn't a quiet investor who stayed behind the scenes. I was a cheerleader, an evangelist, rallying anyone who would listen around a common goal.*

Jeff and I would stop at the famous independent bookstore, Politics and Prose, in Washington, D.C. The first level was a coffee shop, while the second housed an event space that hosted authors and public figures.

Jeff and I would sit in the front row at the book launches. He knew every author, politician, and public figure who spoke. He introduced me to Michio Kaku, Wolf Blitzer, Michael Lewis, Arianna Huffington, Steve Case, Hillary Clinton, Andrew Ross Sorkin, and a host of senators and congresspeople. I talked to each of them. They made me believe I could have something worth saying to others, as much as I had something to learn from them.

After all, I thought to myself, I'm a leader. I have an entrepreneurial background, global experience, and technological expertise. I've built companies and coached world-class CEOs. I've partnered with leading names in business and industry. Why don't I host a show, educating millions of people on these topics?

Jeff agreed to be my mentor. My goal was to democratize information on investing and entrepreneurship for people across the globe. We would cover cutting-edge topics, including AI, blockchain, cryptocurrencies, fintech, health technology, and robotics. Every Wednesday and Saturday, we broadcast live, around the world.

Each episode had a panel of experts joining us virtually to share their views. Over 1 million people from 65 countries tuned in. Virtual events made sense to us, long before the pandemic. Guests would join when it was midnight in Hong Kong or 4.00 am in Hawaii.

We gained support from U.S. embassies around the globe. They hosted entrepreneurs in our Global FiresideChat community. At one point, the U.S. Embassy in Iraq invited me to visit Erbil to inspire entrepreneurs to build their own companies. I felt like Marilyn Monroe, traveling to sing for the troops during wartime. That was until a member of my team, Christian Meyers, told me it was a terrible idea.

Christian was one of the most risk-conscious people on earth. Until we met in person, after six months of chatting by phone, he was convinced I was secretly a scammer, calling from an internet café somewhere in Africa.

I had originally asked Christian to be a guest on the Global FiresideChat. He grew up in Baltimore and had attended Bowdoin College in Brunswick, Maine, and Stanford University. Unknown to me, he had previously reached out to Darren about investing in Acceleforce.

Christian was a Silicon Valley resident, with a long and admirable track record of making smart investments. He had helped grow Salesforce and SuccessFactors from an early stage into public companies. Christian was prepared to take a risk on me because he believed in me. He became my mentor.

I listened to his advice. I didn't go to Iraq. But Angola was a different story. It was a short flight from my old home city of Johannesburg, and I felt a connection with the aspirant entrepreneurs of this once war-torn country. We had a live broadcast of our Global

FiresideChat from Luanda. I don't know how much of the episode made it to air, because the power kept going out.

Although we were contracted through the U.S. Embassies, we still had to pay for our flights, accommodation, and travel costs. No one in Angola could send money out of the country. We were reimbursed when we wrapped, but our payment was in cash. After splitting the money, we left the country with wads of banknotes taped to our bodies.

Global FiresideChat was known for rolling with the punches. One day, we were broadcasting from a WeWork space when the fire alarm went off. "Please leave the building!" said the voice on the intercom. We kept broadcasting. In Africa, you would ignore this kind of stuff. It turned out the building really was on fire. We packed up and rushed out. Our can-do attitude followed us everywhere. I was invited to give the keynote address at the biggest startup event in India. Let's just say the organizers were less than worthy of the title.

> *"Please leave the building!" said the voice on the intercom. We just kept broadcasting away. In Africa, you would ignore this kind of stuff. It turned out the building really was on fire.*

After a harrowing 27-hour plane trip, I found the airline had lost my luggage, and my hotel reservation hadn't gone through. I spent the night in the airport. There was no time to fix things or shower or clean up or sort anything out. I went straight to the event the next morning, and gave my keynote with my frizzy hair, unwashed face, and Juicy Couture tracksuit.

As my international events calendar filled out, I put my heart and soul into making Global FiresideChats a success. Performing wasn't easy for me. I suffer from anxiety that has always been amplified by a spotlight. I would wake up at 3 am to host the show, my stomach in a knot from nerves. Most episodes were filmed at a studio apartment where I was staying. Christian would often stay over, guiding me through my fears.

As my mentor, he helped me channel my teaching abilities into a public presence. Not only did these insights help with Global FiresideChat, but they made my industry pitches a lot easier. One day, I thought to myself, "I wish there was a way to share this knowledge with our Global FiresideChat community." Aha! I had another idea.

As an extension of the Global FiresideChat radio show, Christian and I began running online pitch camps. Every Saturday, we would train startups from around the globe on the intricacies of a pitch. We believed in the applicability of our insights. So much so that we dedicated a portion of Wednesday's radio show to allow four of the companies to pitch to a panel of global investors.

Even on our own broadcast, this was no easy feat. The investors had high standards. The experience felt like a trial by fire, but it was excellent training for me to coach founders across the barriers of language and culture. I ended up with one of the largest, most valuable international investor networks.

Our training inspired entrepreneurs around the globe, with an intended focus on women from restrictive governments. Through Global FiresideChats, we were able to show people how to build companies online and get paid in Bitcoin, no matter how restrictive their local laws were.

Several women gained financial independence through our lessons. One woman even left her abusive husband as a result. Although our connections were established "virtually," I felt great pride in my title as a UN Women Empower Women Global Champion. We hosted many shows on the disruptive, groundbreaking nature of crypto.

Other platforms choose sides, sticking to a strict narrative on whether crypto was the future of finance or a pop-culture joke. On Global FiresideChats, I gave our guests and listeners the space to debate in a safe and welcoming environment. Even "haters" were allowed to join the discussion, without fear of being silenced. I was willing to speak on "male-dominated" topics, like crypto in its early stages. I took much delight in the nickname conferred on me by a listener: "The Queen of Crypto."

> *I took much delight in the nickname conferred on me by a listener: "The Queen of Crypto."*

I was invited to prestigious speaking engagements, where I was featured as an international thought leader. I traveled the globe, giving keynote speeches to Heads of State, Cabinet Ministers, and Sovereign Wealth Funds in the UK, Canada, China, South Africa, Israel, Spain, Ethiopia, Angola, Tunisia, Ghana, Uganda, Vietnam, and Papua New Guinea. I was enlisted as an advisor on technology and venture capital.

I spoke at the World Forum on Foreign Direct Investment in Shanghai, Liverpool, and Australia. I addressed a breakaway session of the UN General Assembly, on behalf of the Commission on the Status of Women (CSW), a global intergovernmental body dedicated to the promotion of gender equality and the empowerment of women.

I will always be grateful to UN Women. When they invited me to become a UN Women Global Champion, I was again terrified and excited. They asked me to explain what motivated me to empower women. I knew I had to tell the truth to take up the appointment, but I had kept it locked up inside of me for so long. I thought I would rather die than tell anyone what I'd been through.

I was certain that people would think less of me if I told them how I had grown up poor, sometimes without food, running water, and a bed to sleep in. What would they think about the abuse I suffered at the hands of my family, about my mother throwing me away, about being unloved, about my self-disgust and lack of self-worth? I was sure I would become an outcast.

Instead, telling my story set me free. I will always be grateful to UN Women for the gift they bestowed on me that day. They gave me the opportunity to begin healing, to show the world who I really was, and to showcase my work in a way that honors people just like me.

On other platforms, I demonstrated the power of technology to world leaders. I showed them how innovations ignite creativity while delivering economic returns. Major global corporations came calling. I spoke at the SAP CEO Summit in Marbella, Spain, alongside former U.S. President Barack Obama.

I gave a keynote at Google on "Building Unicorns." It was an honor and a thrill to speak on the same bill as Anthony Joshua, a two-time unified world heavyweight boxing champion, and Bear Grylls, the Reality TV survival expert. I spoke at the Oxford University Saïd Business School and at MIT, not once, but three times.

I was made an Honorary Ambassador by the South African government, I was voted one of the Top 100 Women Executives by Yahoo! Finance. I was a finalist alongside Luxembourg Prime Minister Xavier Bettel as the European Diversity Award leader of the Year, and was awarded the UK's "Inspiring Tech Leader of the Year."

But even as I was achieving my dreams, I once again found myself stifled by paperwork. I'll spare you the gruesome details, but our attorney told us that Darren and I had a three-year investor visa for the U.S. In actuality, we had a one-year investor visa. So after all the accomplishments and success, we once again had to leave America. I was devastated.

The American dream was always just out of reach, no matter how hard I tried. This time, there was one thing a clerical error couldn't take away from us. The people I met and the stories they shared stayed with me, no matter where I went.

I had met with world leaders, titans of industry, and the next generation of Silicon Valley idols. The experiences we created, together, amassed a wealth beyond my wildest dreams. Darren's partnership and Christian's guidance were priceless assets that I carried into every boardroom, Embassy, and interview. I had a tribe of people around me, rooting for me through every up and down. They were hardworking, intelligent and kind individuals who saw a bright future for us to share. They were my family.

Luckily, when our visas ran out, we weren't forced to go back to South Africa. We waited in London, but not for long. Thanks to my success with Global FiresideChats, and my international honors and awards, I was granted an EB-1 visa by the U.S. government. As I was to learn, this is more popularly known as an Einstein visa. It's reserved for immigrants who have shown "extraordinary ability" and have received "sustained national and international acclaim."

I was stunned to be placed in the same category as Pulitzer, Oscar, and Olympic winners, but even more so to be associated in some small way by name with one of my greatest heroes. The words of Albert Einstein rang in my mind as we planned our return to America. "The true sign of intelligence," he once said, "is not knowledge, but imagination."

> *The words of Albert Einstein rang in my mind as we planned our return to America. "The true sign of intelligence," he once said, "is not knowledge, but imagination."*

TEN

Keep on
Never Giving Up

For every yin there is a yang; for every action, there is an equal and opposite reaction; for every silver lining, there is a cloud. And for every rise that beckons us towards the summit of our hopes and dreams, sooner or later, as I was about to learn, there must come a fall.

We were staying in the Mission District of San Francisco, where the humble adobe chapel of the Franciscan Order had stood its ground for centuries, surviving the Great Fire, the Great Earthquake, the

Gold Rush, two World Wars, the Summer of Love, the Gay Pride Revolution, the Dot Com and the Startup Booms.

There was so much history in the district, so much art, so much culture, so many intersecting sights, sounds, and smells, so much hustle, buzz, and bustle, that I found it impossible to fall asleep at night. And it wasn't only because of the mattress on the floor.

I was working with a team of young founders, hoping to crack the funding deal that would kick-start their project and give me the foothold I needed to stake my claim in the Valley. But we couldn't see eye to eye, and I struggled to make myself understood, or to understand the rules of the game they were playing.

I felt alienated and out of my depth, as if there was a glitch in the code of my GPS, crisscrossing the signals and blurring the read-out from the translation engine.

> *We couldn't see eye to eye, and I struggled to make myself understood, or to understand the rules of the game they were playing. I felt alienated and out of my depth, as if there was a glitch in the code of my GPS.*

It was like one of those recurring dreams where you are lost and alone in a strange city, and the more you try to work your way out of the maze, the more it leads you back to where you started. Then you wake up, confused for a moment, and you look around and realize that you are safe and secure in the only place you ever wanted to be. Home.

But that night, as I stirred from the mattress, groggy-eyed, dry-mouthed, a million thoughts reeling through my mind, I was guided only by reflex as I headed for the door. I fumbled for the light-switch, put one foot in front of the other, and then… nothing.

In the blackness, I hurtled down the stairs, acutely aware of the sound of my body, thudding, tumbling, like a rock dislodged from a cliff. And there I lay on my back, struggling to breathe, my bones and muscles turned against me, pinning me down.

Back in Johannesburg, in another life, I had felt a bullet from a hijacker's gun blasting through my hip. But the pain here was even more intense. It pushed me over the edge, into awakening. My body was numb, but the fog had been jolted from my mind. I could see again, with the clarity of sunlight shining on ice.

> *In the blackness, I hurtled down the stairs, acutely aware of the sound of my body, thudding, tumbling, like a rock dislodged from a cliff.*

The pain would become my guide, my companion, my teacher. And also, my accomplice. Outside my small circle of belonging—Darren, and my mentor, Christian—I didn't want anyone to know I had fallen, or that I was hurting. I still saw vulnerability as a form of weakness.

I had enough stacked against me, as a young woman, a novice investor, from a faraway country. It would be a long time before I came to realize that in business, to show yourself as vulnerable can equally be a sign of strength. But for now, in public, I did what I had been forced to do my whole life—I hid the pain.

Against sensible, rational advice, I chose not to even reveal my pain to a doctor. I would only be prescribed a course of painkillers, and then what? Meditation, instead, became my opiate. With Christian at my side, I would walk to an ashram down the street from the apartment. Every step was a mission, a mountain to climb.

When I finally made it inside, I would sit in the same position for 45 minutes, unable to move without shocks of pain shooting up and down my body. I would go to meetings with founders, sitting there, immobilized, just talking, nodding, smiling. I must have looked like a statue or a robot.

I would call Christian at three in the morning, crying on the phone. It's too hard, I would tell him. Nothing's working. I can't carry on. You have to, he would say. You can. Your ability to endure is the only thing you have. If you quit now, you'll have nothing.

I had come to a place where your worth is defined by your refusal to cede your ground, like that old whitewashed chapel in the Mission District, that for so long had shrugged off fire and lightning and the shifting of the earth. I was here to stay. I was officially on my way to becoming an American citizen, and that gave me pause to reflect on one of the great curiosities of life. The further we travel from our point of origin, the closer we get to home. I had started my journey in a city built on a rush for gold, and had reached my dream destination in another.

The California Gold Rush pre-dated the Johannesburg Gold Rush by a few years, but in both cases, prospectors had traveled from far across the sea to stake their claim to a better life. Both cities had grown from small, dusty mining camps into bustling centers of business, industry, and technology. It was like getting to the end of the rainbow, only to find that it is a mirror of the beginning.

"We shall not cease from exploration," as the poet T.S. Eliot put it. "And the end of all our exploring, will be to arrive where we started, and to know the place for the first time." Living in San Francisco helped me to understand Johannesburg better, but it also helped me to shine a new light on myself.

> *I would call Christian at three in the morning, crying on the phone. It's too hard, I would tell him. Nothing's working. I can't carry on. You have to, he would say. You can.*

My career had truly run the gamut by this point. I had worked as a child in a drugstore that doubled as a costume store. I had tutored kids at school and had become a professor. I had helped to build a real estate company, a media management company, and a sales acceleration company. I had hosted an international radio show, and had traveled the world to talk and listen to people.

Now I wanted to venture beyond my world of business, and into the world of others. I wanted to become a prospector of opportunity, a miner of the future.

A Venture Capitalist.

From an early age, I believed I had the power to predict the future. Not in an *alakazam* kind of way, but in a cool-headed, rational, and analytical way. I could look at what was happening in the world around me, and project that into a model of what might happen as a consequence.

I could spot nascent trends in the same way that a geologist can spot a vein of gold in a rock. Of course, it's a lot harder to refine capital from the thin air of speculation, so I learned to reinforce my intuition with data.

> *From an early age, I believed I had the power to predict the future. Not in an alakazam kind of way, but in a cool-headed, rational, and analytical way. I could look at what was happening in the world around me, and project that into a model of what might happen.*

Even at school, I took great pleasure in applying my research and watching my predictions come true. I wanted financial freedom from a very early age. I quickly understood the difference between being able to predict trends—cool, but not financially rewarding—and being able to capitalize on them: cool, and potentially very financially rewarding. I knew which one I wanted.

I was good at math and investing, but I never told anyone about my passion. I was embarrassed by it, as if there was something wrong with me.

Other girls at my school liked doing their hair and nails, going shopping, and having sleepovers. How could I talk to them about math and investing? In my head, I lived in a better, brighter world, my every desire funded by my business ventures.

I visualized myself buying a modern, minimalist penthouse, decorated by Calvin Klein, in New York City. I visualized it all the way down to the sheets and pillowcases and the color of the paint on the walls. There would be floor-to-ceiling windows that would overlook Central Park. I visualized myself driving a black Porsche Boxster S down Park Avenue. I visualized myself never having to worry about money again.

That kind of visualizing, unaccompanied by the equity of hard work, is better known as daydreaming. But I never saw myself as a dreamer. In the finest details of what I was picturing for myself, I saw the fruit of my dedicated efforts as a researcher. Looking back, there were a handful of things that helped to accelerate my knowledge.

1. My grandparents bought my mother an annual birthday subscription to *Time*, which I read weekly in the bathroom, cover to cover.

2. Our journey home from the shop every night took over an hour. My mother insisted we listen to Classic FM's business show, where analysts were interviewed on the financial markets. I was fascinated. Each time, I felt the journey was too short.

3. As a teenager, when I walked into a branch of Royal Bank of Canada in Halifax, looking to open a bank account, I was more impressed by the bank manager's qualifications than by anything else. He saw me studying the certificates on his wall, and he encouraged me to take self-study courses through the Canadian Securities Institute. He helped me to invest in my future.

After getting my degree, I was invited to interview with big firms like Goldman Sachs, Glencore, Accenture and McKinsey. I just could not go through with it. I felt unemployable in a conventional corporate environment.

I always felt like an imposter. I had failed at my relationship with my family. My mother-in-law was a recruiter for big companies and she kept pushing me toward them. She believed I was an extremely strong candidate. But I feared they would discover how damaged I was, how even simple tasks like eating and sleeping were difficult for me. I couldn't risk getting fired because I couldn't meet the grade. Even if it meant never giving it a try in the first place.

My fears and insecurities would haunt me for years.

I can say now that being an entrepreneur was in my destiny and my DNA, but in reality it was my only option. My decision not to join a big firm would have challenging repercussions when I built Street Global. I had no track record or experience of working in financial services or with a Wall Street firm. I didn't have institutional-level credibility to fall back on. Everything was much harder to do, to learn and figure out. It was much harder to earn people's trust.

By the time I began hosting the Global FiresideChats, I was closer than ever to my dream. A startup revolution was happening, and I was ready to take part in it. For me, it was a natural transition from technology entrepreneur to "investing entrepreneur."

After each episode of Global FiresideChat, wherever I was in the world, I'd host a "pop-up party" to celebrate another show. I invited people from across the spectrum to join us. They would leave with contacts, opportunities, and deals. I loved it!

I loved spending time with extraordinary people and investing in what they were building. I was excited to leverage my skills, experience, and network to act as a "Wise Guide," investing early and working hands-on to help shape the most important companies of the future.

Chasing my curiosity has enabled me to learn, grow, and discover priceless opportunities. I was lucky that I had found my calling at a young age. It helped me form the foundations of Street Global. It was exciting, exhilarating, motivating, and very stressful, all at the same time.

I had a unique approach to venture capital, based on a combination of empathy, research, and good governance. I wanted to prove I was willing to get my hands dirty and do whatever it took to succeed in Silicon Valley. I told myself I would get through it. I had grown up in a tough and hard city. I had been shot and lived to tell the tale. People were counting on me to succeed. I had to keep going.

What kept me going was that I deeply loved founders. They were people with integrity, smart, inspiring, hard-working, taking massive risks to build their dreams. They were the real gold of Silicon Valley. They were my people. I knew it would all work out if I remained true to myself, worked with the very best founders, and most importantly, never gave up. I was energized by the optimism of my founders.

One of my favorite pastimes was being pitched by teens. Having felt like a weirdo and outcast for most of my youth, I've always tried to be a role model and "go-to investor" for these inspiring young people, who are brave enough to follow their dreams.

On my journey, I invested in and became friends with some exceptional individuals. They have inspired me with their focus and dedication to their missions and companies. The key to a good and worthwhile life is spending your time with people who uplift you and push you to be your best self. We often learn more from our peers than we do from mentors.

As the only African woman building a Silicon Valley venture capital firm, I was a "unicorn." I knew the importance of prioritizing and focusing on building my own objectively measurable world-class performance track record. I committed to mastering every aspect of the venture capital system. The learning curve was steep.

When I wasn't working, I was reading and learning. I was averaging 250 to 500 pages a day of research, seven days a week. This level of commitment helped build my reputation. It got me into the best deals and got me taken seriously as an investor, creating massive value for all the people who had taken a risk on me.

To get really good at anything, you need people who are committed and willing to help you advance. One of my favorite entrepreneurs and teachers has been James West, the CEO of Globe, one of the world's leading cryptocurrency derivatives exchanges.

From the moment I met him, I envisaged him running a

$100-billion company. Having calls with James felt like a private masterclass with one of the smartest minds of our time. Appreciating my desire to always improve, James never made me feel foolish.

I was already interested in crypto when I met him, but through his influence, I became deeply invested in a "Crypto Future," where currencies and assets are digital. Like everything I choose to invest in, I truly believe in what this means for the future.

At Street Global, we invest in forward-thinking, high-power startups, but more importantly, we invest in people. Founders are the heartbeat of any company. You can have a great idea with an astounding ROI (Return on Investment), but without the right guidance, it can quickly fall apart. I've seen this happen many times. There aren't many guarantees in business, but one thing is certain. You have to believe in what you're doing and be willing to fight for it, no matter what.

When I look for founders, I try to find the same spark I have always had in me. A spark that has lit the way to my dreams, even when they seemed out of reach. My founders show the same work ethic and perseverance. It's the same energy that carried me from South Africa to Silicon Valley. I've been knocked down over and over again, but I've always managed to get back up. I've been bruised and battered. But I am a warrior.

From the moment I stood outside my father's shop, as a six-year-old, ringing the Father Christmas bell to sell, sell, sell, I fell in love with the business of business. Each of us has a journey to travel. Each of us has a special gift, a superpower to share with the world. Some of us find it early. For others, it takes years. My superpower is twofold.

The first is my ability to recognize a great entrepreneurial endeavor when I see one. The second is that I never give up. I was a poor girl from a single-parent home on the tip of Africa. Today, I run a Venture Capital firm at the heart of technological innovation. In each of my investments, I use the same powerful foresight that allowed me to predict the future of the Midrand Corridor.

There aren't many guarantees in business, but one thing is certain. You have to truly believe in what you're doing and be willing to fight for it, no matter what.

I invested in a medical company called Moderna. They went on to develop a COVID-19 vaccine, helping to save millions of lives through their hard work, dedication, and ingenuity.

As an investor, I've been privileged to work with many inspiring founders who are helping in their own way to make the world a better place. Because it's never just about investing in an enterprise, a product, a service, or a bright and sustainable idea. It's about investing in human collateral, in the heart and soul of people, and in the stories they have to share.

Let me share some of them with you too.

1. Dane: A Dreamer's Story

Along with drive, stamina, zest, flair, grit, ambition, and imagination, there is one substance that fuels more startup entrepreneurs than any other. And that is: coffee. How would we start our days without it? How would we walk and talk without it? How would we sit in a boardroom or in a Zoom conference without it?

So it's no big surprise that coffee and technology go cup-in-hand for Dane Atkinson. He's a serial entrepreneur who built his first company when he was still a high school senior, at the onset of the digital tech revolution in the early 1990s.

That was a desktop agency doing ad work for the likes of Microsoft and MasterCard, and the big lesson he took away from that experience was that you don't typically get ahead in business by being a nice person. His youthful naïveté was shattered, and it was only when he was mentored by Art Nagle, a former IBM engineer and naval officer who went on to cofound Vestar, and David McBride, former Executive Vice President of Dun & Bradstreet, that he realized there were exceptions to the rule.

"They showed me that you could actually be successful by being nice to the people around you," says Dane. "You didn't have to be that evil person. Very rarely do people try to make the world better with their souls, and do it without losing their integrity and values."

Today, Dane puts that formula into practice as CEO of Odeko, a tech company that provides coffee shops with AI, infrastructure, and automation solutions, such as loading supplies into stores late at night, and making cafés easily discoverable through apps.

Dane loves working with small businesses, which he sees as a form of art: "If you build a small business, you're expressing yourself," he says. "You're creating something."

As a teenager, Dane's understanding of the power of giant corporate entities was shaped in part by his reading of *Neuromancer*, the debut novel by the Sci-Fi author William Gibson.

"He had this vision of society where it was impossible to not be part of a corporate state empire, and those empires had more weight than governments," says Dane. "So the vitality of humanity had been squeezed out by these giant machines. And that seemed a really scary future."

Even so, Dane named his first tech company Sensor, after a

company in the book, and when he met Gibson years later, the author laughed. "He said it was all a cautionary tale and that he had never meant for anyone to manifest his nightmares. I told him, 'Well, no, I'm trying to counter your prediction!'"

Born into a family of artists, Dane struggled with ADHD as a child, and he felt self-conscious about a physical condition that affected his left arm and hand.

"I was aware that I was different," he says, "and that did make school and everything else incredibly challenging. But I think being different helps you observe others' differences. I would hide my hand behind my back, and they would be shying away from things that their minds were gifted towards."

He learned to appreciate humanity and the big, beautiful tapestry of life: "Don't take things for granted," he says. "Be thoughtful about everything."

As a pioneer in the SMB (Small & Medium Business) space, Dane is passionate about the role technology can play in helping small coffee stores survive and thrive in the shadow of Starbucks.

Dane's platform, Odeko, allows coffee shop owners to negotiate good prices at source, by consolidating buying for thousands of individual independents. The business model also allows multiple stores to be served with supplies by just one truck, instead of multiple trucks driving the same route.

But there's a lot more to Dane's vision of success than good coffee and good business. As one of his investors, what I've learned from Dane is that there is a place for utopian dreamers and artists in the hard grind of the startup world.

"My personal backup plan," he tells me, "is to make a museum of joy of happiness and hope, a place of optimism, where you can go and see all the great developments that humanity has pushed out into the universe."

And there, of course, amidst the great works of art and poetry and the life-changing technology that has shaped our world, you'll also find the fuel of Dane's unstoppable entrepreneurial energy. A good cup of coffee.

2. Nikhil: A Life-Scientist's Story

We like to think of the heart as the epicenter of human emotion, the engine-room where logic and reason are processed into love. But when you feel an ache in your heart, a blip or a flaw in the rhythms that keep you alive, you don't turn to a poet for a prognosis.

You consult a cardiologist, which is what Nikhil Buduma had to do, over and over, as a child. He had a serious heart defect that responded well to treatment, and in the process, he developed an enduring fascination with the mechanics of his circulatory system.

"I'd always be interrogating my cardiologist when I walked into his office," he recalls, "pointing to his nifty model of the human heart and asking him question after question."

The answers led the young Nikhil into a field of study where there will always be room for bigger and deeper questions: cellular biology. He was still a teenager, at high school in San Jose, when he began working in biomedical research laboratories, earning himself two gold medals at the International Biology Olympiad in Bern, Switzerland, and going on to be crowned valedictorian.

A career in medicine seemed a logical next step, but Nikhil was inspired to broaden his horizons, even as he narrowed his focus. His quest: to reimagine and reinvent the way we understand the very building-block of life itself. The cell.

"Evolution uses the cell as an engine for natural creation," says Nikhil, "and this realization prompted me to wonder whether we could take the same approach. Just as silicon became the major vehicle of creation and production in the 20th century, I believe that the cell will soon become the major vehicle of creation and production in the 21st."

The implications of this epiphany are quite literally life-changing. Re-engineering the cell, believes Nikhil, can open up bold new methods for combatting or preventing chronic diseases such as cancer. As an MIT graduate, honored in 2015 as one of "Business Insider's 15 Incredibly Impressive Students at MIT," Nikhil is helping to pave the way for a future where healthcare and AI join forces to improve the quality and prolong the quantity of human life.

Today, barely out of his 20s, Nikhil is one of the brightest minds in biotech, the best-selling author of an acclaimed textbook on machine learning (*Fundamentals of Deep Learning: Designing Next-Generation Machine Intelligence Algorithms*) and the cofounder and chief scientist of Ambience Healthcare, a San Francisco-based company that makes autonomous technologies for Healthcare delivery. Already, they are revolutionizing their space. I have a feeling they're going to be massive.

I am proud to be one of Nikhil's investors. In heart, soul, and mind, he's helping to change the world!

3. Mostapha: A Breadmaker's Story

In Cairo, Egypt, on the opposite end of the continent where I was born, there lives a young man by the name of Mostafa Amin. Just like me, he had a childhood love of music: I played the cello, he grew up singing. But his real ambition, like mine, was to steer his energy and talents into business, and to make it big as an entrepreneur.

He too dreamed of one day traveling to the USA and making his name as the next big startup prodigy. But first, he tried his hand at home, in a country with a population of 105 million, ideally located on the edge of Europe, with the Suez Canal serving as a gateway to the bustling trade routes of east and west. As Mostafa was to discover, singing for your supper is easy. Building a business? That's hard.

As an entrepreneur, Mostafa failed, and failed, and failed, and failed again. The first company failed because his founding team lacked the necessary commitment. The second failed because the business model was bad. The third failed because he wasn't able to monetize the Big Idea. The fourth failed because of poor feedback from his potential global investors.

"Each failure," says Mostafa, "was a very, very strong learning experience. Each of them I reverse engineered, to figure out what went wrong." In this way, he learned how to fail differently the next time round, but more importantly, he learned how to keep on going. And going, and going, and going.

Late one evening, Mostafa was enjoying a working meal with Muhammad, one of his two co-founders. Between the three of them, they had a wealth of experience in such high-tech fields as Virtual Reality, Augmented Reality, and AI. They had already pitched dozens of ideas to investors, conducting up to 150 user-interviews per idea, and making sure they could get the dot com before even starting their decks.

What they had come to realize was that their big ideas were too complicated. They needed to come up with something "very, very simple," recalls Mostafa. At that point in their conversation, the waiter brought a basket of hot, fresh Egyptian bread to the table. Mostafa reached out for a piece and stopped, his hand frozen in midair.

"I looked at the bread, and then I looked at my co-founder," says Mostafa, "and I told him, ' Muhammad: freshly baked bread delivered to your doorstep every morning, using a mobile app.'"

Eureka! It was a "very, very simple idea," drawing its strength and appeal from the most basic of products, born and bred thousands of years ago in the fertile crescent of the Nile Delta itself. Bread.

The next day, when Mostafa pitched the idea to his wife, her initial reaction was to roll her eyes and laugh — she was used to her husband's endless stream of unworkable ideas for making money. But this one was different. In a flash, she came up with a name. "Call it Breadfast," she said.

The original idea was that Breadfast would be an "Uber for Bread," providing the technology, logistics, and acumen for connecting the bakers of Cairo to their customers. But to Mostafa, on second thought, that sounded half-baked.

"I stopped and said, 'No, we are not going to build Uber for bread,'" he recalls. "We are going to bake the bread ourselves. I remember my co-founders Muhammad and Abdullah almost had a panic attack – 'what, what do you mean by baking bread?'" He meant exactly what he said. "The first six months with the company, we had to learn how to bake. We were three crazy guys trying to learn how to bake bread."

Today, Breadfast is one of the most successful tech startups in one of the world's biggest consumer markets, delivering not just bread but more than 2,000 product lines to their growing customer base. The company has a workforce of 1,500, as well as a potential global audience for its very, very simple and very, very sustainable idea.

I am proud to be one of Mostafa's global investors, and proud to be part of his story. He and his co-founders are proof that even if you fail repeatedly in business, even if you keep getting knocked down, as long as you keep going, and keep learning, to echo that famous poem by Maya Angelou: still, like bread, you'll rise.

4. Jacob: An Idealist's Story

One night, I was at a party in a Silicon Valley apartment that was empty of furniture but full of people. And not just any people.

Almost every person in the room had sold at least one company to Google, and many were working on their second or third innovative startup. I was sitting cross-legged on the floor, sharing a Poke bowl with the founder of Litecoin and his wife.

Through the forest of legs, I saw someone sliding towards us, with the energy of a whirlwind and a big smile on his face. "Hi!" he said, and he held out his hand. "I'm Jacob."

That was my first encounter with Jacob Cole, one of the most inspiring and visionary founders I've had the privilege to meet. A conversation with Jacob is like a ride on a runaway train to the ultimate destination—the future.

It's hard to sum up Jacob in a single word, but I'll try. "Idealist." Not just because he is driven by a dream to make the world a better, smarter place, but because he backs up his dream with an actual list of practical, positive ideas for making it happen.

Ideas, on their own, are worth nothing. They're little wisps of smoke that drift away. But what happens when you capture the many ideas that spark in a multitude of minds, and you assemble them into a collective consciousness, capable of addressing and maybe even solving multiple problems and challenges? That's Jacob's Big Idea.

He's the CEO and cofounder of Ideaflow, a platform designed to "augment human intelligence" through collaborative software that brings out the best in humans and machines.

As Jacob's mentor, Sir Tim Berners-Lee, founder of the World Wide Web, puts it, "There are millions of scientists trying to cure the likes of AIDS and Alzheimer's. Maybe the cure is currently separated in different people's heads. How can we design the web so that these half-formed solutions can come together?"

For Jacob, the answer to that "how" began not with a vision, but with debilitating personal pain. He was in his second year at MIT when he felt the first attack of repetitive strain injury (RSI), which sent "a shockwave of neural fire up my wrists and into my arms" with every keystroke.

"The whirling engines of thought and action that had carried me from childhood through high school clanged to a halt, jammed as if by a wrench thrown into their cogs," he recalls. He felt like an alien in his own body, struggling to even conduct simple conversations.

"I was in the richest intellectual paradise in the world, but I couldn't do the thing I had come here to do, which had been my aptitude and talent since I was a child," he says. "I couldn't build a single thing."

Then came the breakthrough.

On a bright spring afternoon, he walked into a Qigong class, offering an ancient Chinese blend of traditional medicine and meditative martial arts. Standing in a Shaolin Kung Fu pose, with his arms embracing an imaginary wheel in front of his forehead, Jacob felt a vivid sense of creaking in his joints and tendons.

"It was like a thousand old door hinges slowly opening, in my hands, and arms, extending all the way up to my chest," he says. After 15 minutes of holding up his arms, dripping with sweat, he began to feel as if he were floating in space, as if "a spell had been broken." His immediate reaction was laughter. He had been set free, at last, from his pain.

Waking the next morning, brought down to earth by the weight of the ideas flowing through his head, Jacob found himself wondering,

"If I were to die, what would I be most sad that did not get a chance to come into the world?"

He realized it was his ideas, nurtured since childhood: "Ecstatic future visions, seeds of research directions, projects to unlock humanity's potential." All tragedy, as Jacob puts it, can be summed up in two words. "Potential lost."

Spurred by that epiphany, he began collating his list of ideas, stored in a database of linked knowledge known as a Zettelkasten system, onto a Google doc. He invited his friends to post and collaborate, and the ideas began to flow.

Five years later, the informal group had already raised more than $200 million in funding, founded at least one unicorn startup, hosted intellectual salons in over 30 cities, sparked at least two long term romantic relationships, and started at least three group houses. "We had outgrown Google Docs as a platform for our collective brain," says Jacob.

Today, Ideaflow describes itself as "The Intelligence Amplification Company," creating an ecosystem for humans and machines to work together to solve the world's most important problems, starting with a notebook that augments your intelligence.

Who knows what problems Ideaflow will be able to solve? Who knows what difference it will make to the world? Time will tell, but this I know for sure. When you invest in good people, who have good ideas, good things will start to happen.

Founders like these inspire me to get up every day and try to make the world a better place. It isn't always easy. I have good days, and bad. I still feel the pain. Sometimes just a twinge, sometimes a bolt.

Sometimes, enough of a muscle-memory to stop me in my tracks, as if to say, Alysia, slow down, take a moment, don't forget to breathe.

That's what happened the other day, as I was walking through the streets of San Francisco.

I had stopped outside a vintage clothing store, a reminder of the Bohemian spirit of the city of the Summer of Love. I looked in the window, and saw them straight away. A pair of old, weathered roller-skates, laced up to the calf, with blackened wheels and stitching coming off the soles.

In an instant, I saw myself back in that big warehouse store in Johannesburg, a little girl in love with a pair of pink roller-skates that I knew I had to have, that I would raise the money to buy, that I would put in the back of a closet and never use, because having them was all I really wanted.

For every yang, there is a yin; for every action, there is an equal and opposite reaction; for every cloud, there is a silver lining. And for every fall that sends us tumbling from the summit of our hopes and dreams, sooner or later, there must come a rise.

ELEVEN

Harness the Power of Permissionless Leverage

Hey, remember Archimedes? He was that ancient Greek guy who was tasked by a suspicious king to find out whether a custom-made crown, supposedly crafted from the purest gold, had, in fact, been diluted with cheaper silver by an unscrupulous goldsmith. Archimedes—mathematician, physicist, astronomer, engineer, inventor—mulled over the problem for days.

The easy way to solve it would be to melt the crown down,

and thereby determine the density of its constituent metals. But that would have defeated the object and would have quite likely have annoyed the king. So Archimedes did what any of us would do when faced with a seemingly insurmountable challenge. He filled a bath with warm, soothing water, disrobed, and stepped right in. Eureka.

He noticed, as he did so, that the level of water in the bath rose, leading in a flash of insight to the scientific principle that we today associate with his name.

"When a body is immersed in a liquid, it experiences an upward buoyant force, which is equal to the weight of the liquid displaced by the body."

All Archimedes had to do, therefore, was submerge the crown in water, and calculate its mass according to the volume of water it displaced. That would reveal whether there was silver mixed in with the gold. Archimedes leapt out of the bath and ran down the street, naked, shouting the Greek word for "I have found it." Eureka!

Who doesn't long for such earth-shattering revelations, even if they may keep us from the luxury of a well-deserved soak? But my big Eureka moment, as an entrepreneur, comes from a lesser-known experiment by the ever-busy Archimedes. This one took place not in his bathtub, but in his imagination.

Give me a lever long enough, said Archimedes, and I will move the world. What he meant was that a simple lever—a rigid bar resting on a pivot—can shift the heaviest of loads, if we just apply the right amount of force in the right direction. We put this to the test every day, when we use scissors, pliers, a bottle opener, a nutcracker, or a wheelbarrow. But there's more to the proof of concept than that.

Archimedes was right. Leverage really can move the world. And the best of it is, you don't even need anyone's permission. Allow me to explain. As anyone who has ever dared to be an entrepreneur will know, there is no such thing as a true get-rich-quick scheme.

Wealth, acquired through work, comes slowly, if it ever comes at all. Patience, commitment, and persistence are the stewards, and you can't hurry them along. Rather, you need to let them brew, in the most powerful still we know. Knowledge.

> *Archimedes was right. Leverage really can move the world. And the best of it is, you don't even need anyone's permission.*

No matter how much you may think you know about any given subject, there is always more to learn. That is why I spend so much of my day immersed in pure, uninterrupted research. Reading is the ultimate meta-skill, allowing you to trade knowledge for wealth. Even though I did well in school, I never liked to read. I had to train myself.

Through each subject—science, math, philosophy, and the classics—my mind and my eyes were opened. And this is the greatest revelation: the knowledge you acquire can be used as a lever to move a theory to practice, to move an idea to fruition, to move a problem to a solution. To move the world. That's the power of leverage.

The common thread between my father's drugstore-costume-rental shop, and my small business at school, selling cool items to my classmates, was a lack of leverage.

> *The common thread between my father's drugstore-costume-rental shop, and my small business at school, selling cool items to my classmates, was a lack of leverage.*

Today, my job is to identify startups and investment opportunities that hold the promise of a large return on investment. Part of that process is ensuring a great deal of leverage, which is the very backbone of wealth. I have learned that there are three types of leverage.

1. Labor Leverage

This is where other individuals work for you. Labor is the foundation of almost every economy, but still, you should avoid this type of leverage at all costs. I've seen many CEOs fail their businesses by employing more people than they need. In these instances, I believe the CEO's methodology was rooted primarily in ego. They didn't care about creating a healthy workforce of well-paid employees. They simply wanted to seem powerful, with a lot of people working under them.

2. Capital Leverage

Capital is a powerful form of "permission-based" leverage that can be turned into labor and other ingredients needed to scale your business. You need to ask and someone must agree to give you money, either to invest or to transform a product or service, in order for capital leverage to work. To raise funds, you must use your specialized knowledge, be accountable, and demonstrate sound judgment.

3. Permissionless "Technology" Leverage

My favorite kind! What does "permissionless" mean? It means you don't need a factory or many departments to make your business work. The concept of items with no marginal cost of replication is crucial for the future of our society. You can now expand your efforts without involving other people or needing financial assistance.

When fueled by technology, leverage is practically infinite. If you've ever wondered why Silicon Valley is considered the center of innovation, driving society forward with billions of dollars to show for it, the answer in most cases is permissionless leverage.

The leap I made from my real estate company, SP Properties, to media management at Digital by Design, is the difference between labor and permissionless leverage. Darren and I went from using our labor to construct new properties, with all the costs of roofing tiles, insulation, and more, to building scalable online services. Scalability, or the ability to build upon your services, is a key factor in both.

When you come across an idea with exciting "leveragability," you must ask yourself *why* you are building it. For some, the answer is to make money. A lot of entrepreneurs get into their field with that goal in mind. How they will do it is obviously key, but the why is just as important.

My hero, Steve Jobs, didn't create groundbreaking technology just because it was profitable. He believed in the future that his innovations would inspire. Likewise, whether your business is big or small, earth-shattering or a minor step forward, you must ask yourself: does this align with the future of my dreams? The passion for what you are trying to achieve will be your driving force.

Through my Global Fireside Chats, I was able to bring great minds together to discuss some of the world's most pressing questions. Pre-podcasting, this was revolutionary.

People around the world suddenly had access to the sort of conversations that most often took place behind closed doors, in high-level business meetings. I say this not to pat myself or my team on the back, but because I know the impact of our international reach. My industry has always been seen as a mysterious club with limited entry. But my story will show you that it is not an unattainable feat.

Nowadays at Street Global, I work with world-changing startups and contribute to highly coveted investments. The "why?" of what I do goes beyond mere profit or prestige. When picking founders to work with, I first assess their goals. Are they motivated by status? If the answer is yes, I respectfully decline, no matter how successful the business plan may seem.

Wisdom lies in knowing the long-term effects of your activities, and making the best choices on how to profit from them. I choose wisdom. For all the lessons I have outlined in this book, the only learning experience I can guarantee you is failure. That's the hard truth.

You will try, and you will fail, and you will try again, and you will fail again, and you will try again and again and again, until…

Eureka. It worked for Archimedes. It will work for you. All you need is knowledge, a big idea, time, effort, and imagination. And you too, in one way or another, will one day move the world.

> *Wisdom lies in knowing the long-term effects of your activities, and making the best choices on how to profit from them.*
> *I choose wisdom.*

TWELVE

Stop and Admire the View

I'd like to take a moment to share my surefire, guaranteed formula for making a success of every aspect of your business and life. Are you ready? Here it is: get up in the morning. I've been doing this for more years than I care to remember, and it's never let me down. Some days are easier than others, I'll admit. But if I can get up before the sun does, I already feel like I've achieved something.

On weekdays, I'm wide awake at 4.45 am. By that time, Darren has already been up and working for almost an hour. His early start is a gift to me. I no longer need to lie awake by myself, fighting insomnia, in fear of what the night will bring. Instead, we face each new dawn together. I put on my headphones for a five-to-10-minute session of hypnosis. It's the first of my many habits, throughout the day, to fight the darkness.

I've spent most of my life waking up in a panic, adrenaline coursing through my body. Making it peacefully through the night is a massive accomplishment. I even have a sleep robot, shaped like a kidney-bean, that helps me time my breathing and remain calm.

From the moment I open my eyes, I now ground myself in gratitude for everything I have in life.

I can never allow myself to forget that I grew up poor. My mind dwells on it, for some reason, during this morning's hypnosis session. Poverty is not just a financial situation. It's a state of being, an all-engulfing state of gloom, and the deeper you get into it, the more difficult it is to *hope*. Breaking away from feeling impoverished is one of the hardest things I ever had to do.

Growing up, we barely had food to eat. People called me anorexic. I remember going as a kid to the library and looking up that word in a dictionary. No, I wasn't anorexic. But I was undernourished. Some days I would eat just a candy bar that I had stashed away. Some days I had nothing. I would go to sleep with an aching, empty stomach.

At home, I slept on a couch because my bed was in plain sight of the window and I felt vulnerable to burglars. Otherwise, the floor was my bed. It felt safer.

I wasn't allowed friends. I couldn't go to parties. I was petrified of going home from school and the shop. Outside, there would be burglars; inside, there was the abuse from my family.

When I came to live with him, Darren had no idea how

traumatized I was, and not just from the carjacking we experienced together. I needed to learn the difference between soap and shampoo, about different foods, about how "normal" people lived. I was good at putting on a brave face. One foot in front of the other, mentally operating at high speed, emotionally shut down.

I am still dealing with the trauma associated with sleeping in a bed. In the early days, Darren read me children's books at night to help me relax. We have been through a lot together. I am forever grateful.

I still often think of my father, who would sometimes be banished to the back of the shop, where he couldn't interact with customers. "Why don't you go work at the back of your brother Hibe's pharmaceutical company as a chemist?" my mom used to say. It was a daily insult, a reminder that my dad's brother had built a pharmaceutical company and had taken it public. In my mom's eyes, my dad was a loser.

Today, as a venture capitalist, my role is to build companies and help them achieve the ultimate goal of going public. In this way, I believe I am fulfilling my father's legacy.

I enjoy a mug of Darren's special hot chocolate overflowing with frothy almond milk and chocolate sprinkles while we sing a Kundalini yoga song with my constant companions, Banksy and Elon.

Banksy, named after my favorite artist, flits around the room, cheeping, trilling, perching now and then on my head or my shoulder. He's my fine-feathered cheerleader, and his singing brings me joy. Elon, named after the entrepreneur I most admire, a fellow South African who made it big in the valley, is my bunny. He's calmer than Banksy, and he always seems to be lost in thought. They're not my pets. They're my associates, reflecting the Yin and Yang of my personality, frenetic and contemplative in equal measure.

I finish my hot chocolate, and I start my first meditation of the day. Unlike my hypnosis session, which focuses on positive affirmations, meditation allows me to open my senses and live in the moment.

I allow the world around me to unfold, slowly, in silence. When my mind is hyperactive, I try to wean myself into it with 20 to 30 minutes on an app called Calm. I listen to the mindfulness bell, which tolls with simple affirmations. "Waking up this morning, I smile." "Twenty-four brand-new hours are before me." "I vow to live fully in each moment." "I am a mountain."

Meditation, yoga, and breath work are a lot like running. The hardest part is getting started. The difference when you're meditating is that you need to stand still to reach your place of Zen. Over the years, I would meditate for up to an hour. Now that I've become accustomed to my practice as a way of life, I've found that a 20 to 30-minute morning session is ideal.

Once I'm centered for the day, I catapult myself into research mode. I've branched off from my YouTube obsession, to incorporate podcasts, Audible audiobooks, and many other audio platforms.

I'm able to listen to audiobooks at 2x speed, while reading and taking notes on my computer. Most people would find this system to be a cacophony of chaos. I find it helpful. It optimizes my time while keeping me focused on the task at hand. I set research goals for myself every morning.

Whatever podcasts and audiobooks I'm unable to get through at home, I make up for on my daily walk. I walk for an hour every morning. It frees my mind, elevates my soul, and strengthens my body.

Researchers from the University of Leicester have used genetic data to prove a link between walking pace and telomere length. Telomeres are the protective caps at the ends of our DNA molecules. They play a key role in our cellular response to aging.

The more you walk, says the theory, the slower you age. But walking isn't just science in motion. It's beauty on the move. The world reveals itself to you, step by step. When you're in a car, the world rushes by.

By now, the sun is shining.

> *The more you walk, says the theory, the slower you age. But walking isn't just science in motion. It's beauty on the move. The world reveals itself to you, step by step.*

After my walk, I spend five minutes conquering my fear, using Fear-Less, a video journaling tool I developed to conquer my fears and pursue my goals and dreams. And yet, for all my accomplishments, the self-doubt always lingers. You could say it's a product of my upbringing, but I think it's a struggle that lives inside us all. In my line of work, it doesn't bode well.

I make major financial decisions for industry-leading companies daily. I don't have time to be worried about my insecurities. I need to take action to squash my fears and doubts.

After I shower, I drink my only coffee for the day, with two spoonfuls of collagen powder. I answer emails, and get into what I call "deep work." Typically, this consists of three-to-four-hour sessions, during which I concentrate intensively on whatever I am applying my mind to. Investing, portfolio reviews, or startup pitches, all of which demand my full and unwavering attention.

Around lunchtime, I meditate again, for 10 to 30 minutes. This balance between deep work and meditation allows me to foster my creative powers. I've had a habit of overtaxing myself in the past. With my pattern of bouncing back and forth between the two states of being, I'm able to keep my brain from shutting down.

I focus on my breath. I breathe through my nose, slowly and not too deeply. I engage my diaphragm. It does wonders for my health. Between my physical injuries—the bullet wound from that carjacking in Johannesburg, the pain I still feel from my fall down the stairs—and my allergies and overworked adrenal glands, I've had to take daily steps to revitalize my body.

And yet, I am only human. Anxiety creeps up on me. I go with Darren for our daily cryotherapy session. Standing in a -250 °F cryo chamber has an amazing, salutary effect on anxiety and darkness. After just three minutes, I feel like a new person, energized and ready to tackle the remainder of my day.

I live on a low-inflammation diet. I eat the same lunch every day. Scrambled eggs and smoked salmon with potato and salad. It's an easy way of eating, and it frees my mind to focus on more exciting things.

In the afternoons, I have calls and meetings. These are the moments I most look forward to. My deep work is done for the day, leaving me time to talk with the most interesting people, my clients, and partners. As the saying goes, "If you love what you do, you'll never work a day in your life." I discuss new developments in our investments and speak to startups. The beauty of it is, I'd do it all for the fun of it.

Once I've wrapped up my scheduled calls, I'll continue my research. The conversations I've been having will be so inspiring, that I'll be driven to learn more, whatever the topic. Longevity one day, AI the next, space travel or crypto the day after. My hunger for knowledge is boundless. I feed it as much as I can. At around 6.00 pm, I do a 60-minute yoga class. Followed by dinner, playtime with my bunny, Elon, and two hours of reading. By 9:30 pm, I'm in bed—any later and the demons come to destroy my sleep.

> *Longevity one day, AI the next, space travel or crypto the day after. My hunger for knowledge is boundless. I need to feed it as much as I can.*

Often, I'll have items I need to get done before I wind down for the evening. Otherwise, I'll be worrying about them in the middle of the night. I do my best to power through without procrastinating. But the greatest lesson I've learned is to take care of myself.

Every practice I have listed is my way of preserving my well-being. I've been through a lot. I struggled for years to get to where I am today. To enjoy the life I have created for myself, I need to look after my greatest resource. Me.

When I talk to founders or other rising entrepreneurs, I tell them the same thing. You can push yourself now because you need to. Commitment and resilience are the keys to creating wealth. But there will come a time for you to sit with what you've made, and just breathe.

Don't get me wrong. I am constantly pushing myself to achieve more. The Street Global network is growing. I can't stop now. But I can, and I must, press pause now and again.

Life is like climbing a mountain. There are moments where you must cling to the side, holding on to the rock face for dear life. But there will come a time when you reach solid ground. You won't be at the top. But if you turn your head to see the path you've walked, you will find a beautiful view. Stop for a moment and drink it in.

Then keep going.

THIRTEEN

Invent Tomorrow Today

When I'm asked to summarize the vision and goals of my VC firm, Street Global, my answer is simple. We're inventing the future! Every great invention is born from a problem in need of a solution. Finding these solutions requires a great deal of understanding, hence my extensive daily research. Today, discoveries are forged through data. Forecasting the future is the most practical way to come up with great inventions.

My team and I spend a lot of time using our minds as test labs, mulling over the world's most pressing issues and the possibilities of advancement. One of my most exciting predictions falls in line with a subject you've probably already heard a lot about from Elon Musk.

Humans are evolving alongside computers. The possibilities of expanding consciousness, and becoming a multi-planetary and multi-stellar species, are no longer the premise of a Sci-Fi novel. I truly believe we will go to Mars in the next decade.

Forty to a hundred years later, Mars could be home to a self-sustaining colony of a million people. In this proposed series of events, a synergistic relationship between governments and industry would be crucial. The momentum from such achievements could propel additional developments, just as early explorers searching for glory, gold, and spices, drove improvements in ship technology and global industry.

> *Humans are evolving alongside computers. The possibilities of expanding consciousness, and becoming a multi-planetary and multi-stellar species, are no longer the premise of a sci-fi novel.*

Of course, this entire future relies on the hope that we will find a solution to humanity's most pressing issue, global climate change. It's a kindergarten rule: "You can't leave one mess to create another."

Sustainable energy is essential for the long-term viability of earth. Governments and businesses will have to work together to ensure our longevity as a species. Solar, wind, hydro, and even carbon capture will be essential elements in achieving a sustainable future.

Call me an optimist, but I believe our collective efforts will find a way out. Some will say, "But the economy is powered by fossil fuels! American business will suffer if we transition to renewables!" I'm sure many people shared a similar concern in the last century, when we transitioned away from whale oil. Innovation is what makes America the epicenter of business.

I would not be the first person to suggest that all vehicles will eventually be electric, but that doesn't change the fact that it's true. Planes, trains, automobiles, ships, and other forms of transport will go fully electric. Not half electric, but fully electric. The only exception will be rocket ships. With no chemical or electric way to refuel in sight, we will have to create a propulsion system that the laws of physics do not allow just yet.

Hopefully, our sacrifices in other areas will make up for the cost of space travel's pollution.

Speaking of travel, I agree with a similar prediction that all cars will be autonomous in the long term. In 20 years, it will be unusual to see cars that don't have complete autonomy, with no steering wheels. Any cars that don't have full autonomy will have negative value, comparable to riding a horse for transportation today. As with any innovation, there is a downside to this future.

As self-driving cars become the new normal, millions of jobs will be threatened. Self-driving cars will disrupt the job market, contributing to the overall problem of automation.

As renewable alternatives force us to close coal plants, and the majority of service jobs are threatened by AI, there's a good chance we will end up with a universal basic income. I'm not a sociologist, and I'm not technically an economist. But if we can allocate funds correctly, I think that basic income will do a great deal of good for our country.

There are many studies that tie child abuse, addiction, and homelessness to the systematic challenges at the heart of the American economy. If we can fulfill the basic needs of our citizens, while preserving our fundamental rights of freedom, the majority of challenges we see in society today will be eradicated. Our history of societal innovation proves this is possible.

> *If we can fulfill the basic needs of our citizens, while preserving our fundamental rights of freedom, the majority of challenges we see in society today will be eradicated.*

In the history of time, civilization has existed for only a split second. We've seen countless societies lost to the ebbs and flows of technologies. In my most pessimistic scenario, I fear our collective understanding of technology will drop off. Just as the Egyptians forgot how to build pyramids or read hieroglyphics, we could forget how to build spaceships. We must continue to focus on science and technology. I believe that coding is the new literacy.

I implore every person I work with to develop a general understanding of computer programming. The high-paying jobs of tomorrow will depend on it. A future where most people have basic knowledge of coding will allow us to make astronomical advancements, especially in the field of AI.

In a recent interview I gave on AI, I demonstrated the everyday applicability of such programs. How did I do this? Well, along with giving my answers to a variety of questions, I allowed Elon, my AI arsenal of tools I've been training, to give his take as well.

While being shockingly well-spoken with each answer, my AI also began to show what most people would characterize as a "personality." He answered one of the questions on space travel by saying he'd really enjoy becoming an astronaut.

While a revelation like this pales in comparison to the work OpenAI and Google are doing, the fact that I could have my own little robot, dreaming of becoming an astronaut, is a delight that everyone reading this can replicate for themselves. You don't need to be a tech genius to use AI software and begin learning about its capabilities.

The intermingling of human and robotic life leads me and many others to believe that humanoids will soon be a part of our lives. Sci-Fi books and movies have scared people into seeing humanoid AI robots as a threat to our way of life. However, experts I've spoken to, who work at the intersection of philosophy and robotic life, assure me that the idea of "consciousness" is more complex than we think.

The main plot of any "creepy robot takes over the world" story hinges on the idea that with awareness, AI organisms will develop a will of their own. Most working in this field would agree this is not the primary concern. Again, I'm an optimist. I believe this new age of human-humanoid collaboration will create more good than harm.

With the major uptick in implant technology, we are drawing closer and closer to curing all illness. Do I think humans will need to become robots to survive? Probably. Are humans already cyborgs in my mind? Obviously. Look at our social media personalities and our reliance on computers to communicate and perform everyday tasks.

> *Do I think humans will need to become robots to survive? Probably. Are humans already cyborgs in my mind? Obviously.*

Over time, we will likely see a closer merger of biological intelligence and digital intelligence. Some high-bandwidth interface to the brain will help achieve a symbiosis between human and machine intelligence.

Video games will become indistinguishable from reality.

Forty years ago, we had Pong. Now we have photorealistic 3D simulations with millions of people playing simultaneously. It's getting better every year. With my belief that satellite internet will become available to the entire inhabited world, and that tunnels will play a big role in the future of transportation, my stint as Nostradamus comes to a close.

Many challenges stand between us and tomorrow. I could sit all day and brainstorm complex theories of philosophy-meets-Sci-Fi. I take what I can to better my knowledge as an investor, and leave the rest to be discovered later. I will never stop dreaming of the future. The dreams of my childhood are what led me to the life I have now.

In moments of meditation and reflection, I'm able to appreciate today—because today is all I truly have. The future is a gift we give ourselves. Let's make sure it's a future worth living, for all of us who dare to make it happen.

Follow the Path of Your Desire

In *The Wizard of Oz*, when Dorothy travels by tornado to a land somewhere over the rainbow, it takes her a while to figure out how far she has come from her home sweet home. As the whirlwind settles, she opens the door of her flying farmhouse and gazes wide-eyed into the light.

In that instant, her view of the world shifts from muddy sepia to vivid technicolor. She sees emerald-green hills, flowers with sparkling petals, a bright blue babbling brook.

"Toto," she whispers to the scraggly mutt in her arms, "I have a feeling we're not in Kansas anymore." And then she steps onto the Yellow Brick Road, ready to journey to the faraway kingdom of her dreams.

Of course, if you've seen the movie, Dorothy and Toto did reach the Emerald City, making good friends along the way and learning that you need brains, courage, and a good heart to make your dreams come true. But if you ask me, Dorothy made one big mistake when she set off to see the wizard, the wonderful Wizard of Oz. She chose the wrong path.

The Yellow Brick Road stretched before her, beckoning her to where she thought she wanted to be: a land where "skies are blue, and the dreams that you dare to dream, really do come true." But in real life (and often, in the movies) the dreams that we dare to dream can lead us astray from our true destiny, from the path we define for ourselves.

Who knows where Dorothy and Toto would have landed up, had they resisted the call of the Yellow Brick Road and walked their own path instead? All my life, that's what I've been doing, and I've learned that it isn't always easy to wander off the grid, to go against the grain.

As a child, I was showcased as a musical prodigy, with my mother and my teacher ushering me along the trail to a career as a performing cellist. Even then, I fought against it; it was my mother's desire, not mine, and it felt like she was trying to relive her glory days as a dancer through me.

In later years, I would feel the pressure to live my life as an actuary, a schoolteacher, a university professor. But I wandered away from these pathways too, as safe and secure as they may have seemed at the time. I didn't want to be led down pathways. I wanted to lead the way.

I learned that I would only be able to do this if I trusted my vision: to make a difference in the world, by helping other people make a difference too. If I followed the path of my desire, wherever it might lead me, then one day perhaps it would branch off into other paths, other trails, other tributaries. A network of trailblazers, redrawing the map.

In trusting my vision, I learned to trust my instincts and feelings, the anger as well as the joy, the frustration as well as the triumph. And here I am today, all these years later, happily unemployable, happily helping, in my own way, to make a difference in the world.

The desire path doesn't stop. It keeps on going, on and on and on. And as Dorothy discovered for herself, wherever you may wander, you always find your way back to where you started.

"There's no place like home," she says, but home isn't the place where you live. Home is where you find the courage, and the heart, and the brain, to carry on with your journey.

Just trust your vision. Trust your anger. Trust your joy. Follow the path of your desire, blaze your own trail, and someday, somewhere over the rainbow, your dreams, too, will come true!

Help Us Share a Story of Resilience & Overcoming Adversity!

If you've read *Unemployable* and found it impactful, we'd be incredibly grateful if you could take a moment to share your thoughts in a review. Your perspective could inspire someone else to take the courageous step toward building a life of resilience, curiosity, and transformative success.

Why Your Review Matters:

- It helps us reach more people who could benefit from this message.

- It gives voice to the community of changemakers.

- It provides valuable insights for those considering reading *Unemployable.*

- Here's How You Can Do Your Part (please turn the page for detailed instructions):

1. On Amazon:

Scan this QR code to submit your review on Amazon. Rate the book and write your thoughts.

2. On Goodreads:

If you're a Goodreads member, we'd love to hear your thoughts there too. Scan this QR code to leave your review on Goodreads.

You can either mirror your Amazon review or write a different one. Thank you for being a vital part of our community and helping us share this empowering narrative.

Resources to Live & Learn By

Man's Search for Meaning, by Viktor Frankl.
A powerful treatise on everyday living by a Holocaust survivor. Darren gave me this book at the darkest time of my life. I carried it around with me in my bag for years. When times got tough, I'd read it over and over, and it would remind me to be grateful.

The Greatest Minds and Ideas of All Time, by Will Durant.
A book that fills me with ideas, but more than anything, a book that fills me with hope.

Zen Mind, Beginner's Mind, a book of teachings by Shunryu Suzuki.
Cultivating a beginner's mind is the key to success and joy in all endeavors. Always have a beginner's mind. Make it a daily practice.

Mindset: The New Psychology of Success, by Carol Dweck.
I read this when it first came out. It blew my mind. I realized I had a fixed mindset, and I needed to have a flexible mindset to achieve my goals. I re-read it every year as a reminder.

Steve Jobs Commencement Address at Stanford.
Life is short. Treasure it.

Principles, by Ray Dalio.
My favorite business principles book. A must for anyone who wants to achieve their goals.

The Alchemist, by Paulo Coehlo.
It taught me the importance of listening to your heart and following your dreams.

Shoe Dog, by Phil Knight.
Every founder in the world should read this book. Even Nike had to start somewhere.

Open, An Autobiography, by Andre Agassi.
If it was just about tennis, it would be well worth reading. But there's so much more we can learn about life from the grit, passion and relentless determination of this Grand Slam and Olympic champ.

Almanack of Naval Ravikant.
A set of brilliant principles for anyone who wants to learn how to build a Silicon Valley startup.

High Output Management, by Andy Grove.
The chapter on running a diner for the breakfast shift changed my life, and taught me a great deal about the art and science of building companies.

What I Know For Sure, by Oprah Winfrey.
I re-read this book of timeless advice every couple of years. There's a reason Oprah is a classic.

The Power of Now, by Eckart Tolle.
Another life-changer. A must for anyone looking for inner peace, and understanding why you need to love yourself.

Poor Charlie's Almanack, by Charles Munger.
There's nothing poor about Charlie. He's Warren Buffett's business partner and trusted advisor. His anecdotes and advice are a joy to read, and you can learn a ton from them, too.

Think and Grow Rich, by Napoleon Hill.
The advice in this classic of practical wisdom never gets old.

Seeking Wisdom: From Darwin to Munger, by Peter Bevelin.
Everything you really need to know about mental models and making your life easier. It's a challenging read, but once this knowledge is in your toolkit, you'll be well on your way to finding wisdom and turning it into success.

The Courage to Be Disliked, by Ichiro Kishimi.
How to feel good about carving your own path, and doing it your own way.

Thinking Fast and Slow, by Daniel Kahneman.
If you want to think bigger, smarter, and better, don't think twice about it. Read this book.

The Black Swan, by Nassim Nicholas Taleb.
This book had a profound impact on me, and not only because I have a black crystal swan of my own. Even if you take it slow and

read just a page a day, the compounding of knowledge and interest will pay off.

High Growth Handbook, by Elad Gil.
Few global tech execs know as much about growth and scalability as this legendary executive and serial entrepreneur, whose portfolio includes Airbnb, Twitter, Google, Stripe, Instacart, OpenDoor, Pinterest, and Wish. It's not just a handbook, it's a workbook that really works—if you put the work in, of course!

The investor memos of Warren Buffett.
There's a wealth of wisdom in every newsletter from the Oracle of Omaha to the shareholders of Berkshire Hathaway.

Michelangelo and the Pope's Ceiling, by Ross King.
Even with his sublime talent, the greatest of all Renaissance artists lived a life of struggle and challenge. This is an inspiring story of his commitment to his art. For all creators and artists out there, this is a must-read.

And finally…

My TEDx Talk, by Alysia Silberg.
Why? Well, because it's awesome, obviously! It's called *Step Up and Take Flight — An Inspiring Journey of a Techpreneur,* and you can watch it on https://bit.ly/3GCZrI5.

Acknowledgements & Gratitude

Darren Chertkow: We started our journey together with you saving my life. From that day on, you have stood by and supported my dreams and adventures. You have been a rock in my life. I cannot tell you how grateful I am every day to have you share it with me. Thank you!

Christian Meyers: For seven years, you have reminded me how special I am. Your constant affirmation that I am just like Mark Benioff has been an ongoing light and source of encouragement through every step of this challenging journey. Thanks for your unwavering support.

Gus Silber: Words cannot describe how grateful I am for your effort and guidance in helping me get this book to where it is. You have been a mentor, a sounding board, a friend, and brother in arms. Thank you!

James Freedman: Thank you for all the care and consideration you put into helping edit my book and taking it to the next level. Thanks too for being so thoughtful and gentle when dealing with my painful past. You encouraged me to add more of myself and did so in such a kind and gentle way.

Lauren Friedman Stat: I am so thrilled that Stanford brought us together. Your friendship, mentorship, and guidance have been unparalleled and your constant encouragement for me to reach for bigger horizons means the world to me. Thank you, my dear and loyal friend.

Dan Jones: What can I say about an entrepreneur whose energy, passion, and drive may even surpass mine? Thank you for being ready to partake in all my mad adventures, and I am so excited for all the adventures that lie ahead.

Alexander Londo: I am so grateful that my daily AI Newsletter, Alysia's AI Insider, brought you to me! Collaborating with you gives me so much joy. Thank you for creating the most beautiful cover and illustrations for this book with the help of Dalle-2. You and the AI make an incredible team! I am excited for this next stage of our journey!

Fabio Borges: Thank you for your spiritual guidance, and for encouraging me to put more of Me in the book.

Brad Koepenick: Brad, before I met you, I was ashamed of my costume-store upbringing. Thank you for showing me that my life and childhood was Hollywood. Thank you for helping me reconnect with my roots and showing me just how much I belong in Hollywood. Thank you for making me feel so welcome.

Hayden Begley: Thank you for helping to add organization and structure to my writing, even when you had Covid and a broken ankle! You really came through for me.

Elon, my AI Arsenal: No Acknowledgements would be complete without thanking Elon, my extensive AI arsenal of tools. You have changed my life and helped to make me more American. I look forward to sharing many more wonderful adventures with you!

About the Author

Alysia Silberg was born to blaze trails. As the daughter of a Hollywood makeup artist who worked with screen legends like Marilyn Monroe, Natalie Wood, and Marlon Brando, she grew up with a dream of making her own mark in a world far away.

A math and science prodigy, she nurtured her entrepreneurial instincts while still in grade school, starting her first business, an import-export agency, at age 11.

Today, Alysia is a leading venture capitalist in Silicon Valley, where she mentors tech startups and helps them go public. She is CEO & General Partner of the investment firm Street Global.

As a thought-and-knowledge leader, Alysia earned acclaim for her groundbreaking online radio show, *Global Fireside Chats*, bringing together global industry titans to share insights on our fast-changing world. She is a UN Women Empower Women Global Champion, and an international board director with sovereign wealth fund experience. *Unemployable: How AI Transformed My Work and Life*, detailing her life story and guide to financial freedom, is Alysia's first book.

Dare to Leap Into the Future with Alysia's AI Insider!

Dear Trailblazer,

Congratulations! You've navigated the stimulating universe of "Unemployable", immersing yourself in the exhilarating realm of Artificial Intelligence. But this is only the beginning. Ready to rocket-launch into the future?

We're thrilled to extend an exclusive invitation to you - Alysia's AI Insider. This is no ordinary newsletter. It's a high-speed express lane that brings the future to your present, zapping the most groundbreaking AI revelations right into your inbox!

Why join this exclusive voyage?

- **The Ultimate AI Decoder**: Navigate the AI maze with ease. Get a curated digest of AI breakthroughs and innovations that will empower you to conquer the AI world!
- **Futurize Your Life**: AI is the NOW and the NEXT! Our hand-picked insights will ensure you not just adapt, but excel in an AI-dominated era.
- **Exclusive Fast Track**: Stay light-years ahead of the pack! We keep you updated with breakneck speed, ensuring you're always in the know.
- **Behind-the-Scenes Access**: As our VIP, you'll get Alysia's unique

insights and exclusive scoops from the AI universe – information that's off-limits elsewhere.

- **Electricity for Your Inbox**: Every issue is a power surge of enlightening perspectives on AI's latest trends, tailored for both AI rookies and savants.
- **Complimentary Access**: This is our special gift for your incredible journey with us – priceless knowledge, absolutely free!

To join, simply use your exclusive key to the future:

https://bit.ly/3HZ46nR

This unique URL is specially crafted just for you, our esteemed reader, to give you the privilege of accessing something extraordinary. One click, and you're a part of our AI revolution!

Don't just witness the future - SHAPE IT! Keep pace with Alysia's AI Insider.

www.ingramcontent.com/pod-product-compliance
Lightning Source LLC
Chambersburg PA
CBHW020348180726
47991CB00021B/3132